WHAT PEOPLE ARE SAYING ABOUT DRENDA KEESEE...

It's quite rare to find the combination of truth teller, confidante, and easy laugh in one person, but Drenda Keesee brings it, which is why she is beloved by so many, including me.

—*Anita Renfroe*
Comedian and author

Anyone with a family knows how challenging it can be. Drenda brings such a fun and fresh perspective on how to do life with family well.

—*Lisa Bevere*
Co-founder, Messenger International; best-selling author

The Keesee family is precious to me. They have trained their children to be godly and loving, and that's the way our families should be.

—*Dodie Osteen*
Co-founder, Lakewood Church

You can tell a lot about a couple by looking at their family, and the Keesee family is a true testament to that. Not only do Gary and Drenda's children love to spend time with their parents, they are also heavily involved in their ministry—they don't just have fun together, they work together. Through their effective parenting, they have built a strong family model for their community.

—*Tina Konkin*
Co-founder, R3 Lifeline; relationship counselor

I have known Gary and Drenda Keesee and their family for sixteen years now. They have been forerunners in the area of family and have done family well. Their ministry has spanned into a global ministry encouraging others to do family God's way. This book is timely and vital; read it and then let it change you!

—*Leif Hetland*
Author, *Seeing Through Heaven's Eyes*

Jesus said, "You will know them by their fruit" (see Matthew 7:20), and Gary and Drenda have demonstrated such good fruit in the lives of their own children. In the midst of a secular society that continually degrades what the family is all about, it's clear to see that the godly upbringing and standards by which they raised their children should be used as a shining light example for the whole world to see. The proof is in the pudding.

—*Andrew Ironside*
Lecturer and trainer, Hillsong Leadership College

Drenda is one of the most empathetic yet fun parents we know. She has the joy of the Lord on her even when family life does not look so joyful. You will learn about effective family ground rules that work.

—*Mary Hudson*
Author, *Joyful Parent = Happy Home*

NASTY
GETS US
NOWHERE

WOMEN & MEN SUCCEEDING TOGETHER

DRENDA KEESEE

WHITAKER
HOUSE

Nasty Gets Us Nowhere
Women and Men Succeeding Together

Faith Life Now
P.O. Box 779
New Albany, OH 43054
1-(888)-391-LIFE
www.FaithLifeNow.com

ISBN: 978-1-64123-505-1
eBook ISBN: 978-1-64123-506-8
Printed in the United States of America
© 2020 Drenda Keesee

Whitaker House
1030 Hunt Valley Circle
New Kensington, PA 15068
www.whitakerhouse.com

Library of Congress Cataloging-in-Publication Data (Pending)

1 2 3 4 5 6 7 8 9 10 11 ᴡ 27 26 25 24 23 22 21 20

CONTENTS

FOREWORD

John and Lisa Bevere

Lisa: Men and women were never meant to compete with each other… they were always designed to complement one another. I wish I had known this truth in the early years of my marriage to John. Those first few years were harder than they needed to be. How sad!

John: I also wish I had known this truth early in our marriage. I would frequently throw out the "submission" card, attempting to enforce my position and authority. This did not go well with Lisa—and rightfully so! We're both strong-willed and passionate people. I can't forget to mention that we're both Italian—and neither of us enjoys being trampled upon.

Lisa: Things shifted when John began to view me differently. He began to express, "Lisa, I'm the leader…but I can't do this without you." Submission, an often-misrepresented word, says we are two people under the same mission. John and I realized we were two people under the same mission, who needed each other. We are allies, not enemies.

John: The reality is, we all have missions in life. Lisa and I have a mission as a couple, as parents, and as grandparents—and please, for clarity, we like to be referred to as G-Daddy and G-Momma! The world will know Jesus is real when we love and work well with one another. This should be the joint goal of all men and women, whatever their season or occupation. Let's face it, aren't we all (not just men) ministers of reconciliation—God's ambassadors to the lost? (See 2 Corinthians 5:19–20.) God uses us to persuade men and women to drop their differences and enter into God's work of making things right between them.

Lisa: John and I have a goal that every year, our marriage grows in love, respect, and honor—and by the time we take a final breath, we will be more in love than the day we met. We have a mission to raise children who will glorify God with their lives. We have a mission as G-parents and leaders to position others to go farther than we've gone ourselves.

John: Submission is about two people becoming better together than they could've ever been on their own. Each of us has contributions that add value and strength to one another. Both Lisa and I have witnessed our marriage flourish when we've dropped our differences and united around our strengths. The same can happen for you!

Lisa: Yes! John and I know very well from experience that *Nasty Gets Us Nowhere*! That's why we are thrilled that our dear friend Drenda has written this book. Whether it's spouses, family members, or coworkers, men and women can succeed together! The truths found in this message will provide you with the tools you need to build a healthy and thriving marriage so you can stop competing and begin complementing one another.

We're truly better together!

—*John and Lisa Bevere*
Best-selling authors
Co-founders, Messenger International

INTRODUCTION

Gary Keesee

It is an honor and a privilege to be asked to contribute to Drenda's new book, *Nasty Gets Us Nowhere*. Drenda and I have been married and working together for the last thirty-eight years, and the results have been amazing! We have rarely spent a day apart over that time period and have learned how to use our differences as an advantage and strength in any situation. I need Drenda and she needs me; together, we have found that men and women working together is the winning combination that God designed.

Unfortunately, we live in a culture that is doing all it can to redefine family, marriage, and even gender. The results of such foolishness can be predicted and are playing out before our eyes with tragic consequences. Drenda tackles these politically charged topics head-on with statistics and data to back up her analysis as well as her own journey through the haze of feminism and abortion that she went through in her younger years. She is now on a mission to dispel the lies and help both men and women find out who they really are.

Today, Drenda is a very successful business owner, a television personality on her own daily TV broadcast, *Drenda*, and a sought-out speaker and life coach. You will find her candor entertaining as well as riveting as she speaks from her experience and heart to today's generation. Drenda's enthusiastic zeal for life has earned her the nickname "Miss Sure You Can." And whether you are a man or woman, young or old, you will find that *Nasty Gets Us Nowhere: Women and Men Succeeding Together* inspires and answers many questions of the day.

Drenda's passion is to see you live the good life, the happy life that God has designed for you to live. She wants you to know that it is not too late for you no matter where you find yourself today. And I know that if she ever had the chance to meet you in person, she would look you in the eye with a smile and say, "Sure you can!"

—*Gary Keesee*

1

IS THIS THE END?

I looked in disgust at my reflection in the mirror as tears streamed down my cheeks. *My dad was right; I have a nose like a banana*, I thought, remembering something my father said to tease me. *Who could ever love me?*

My blonde hair was cut short, so short it barely covered my ears. I had a gray tie hung around my neck, not because it was part of my high school uniform or just fashionable, but because I was making a *statement*.

That's what a *strong* woman looked like. And *I* was a strong woman.

As I studied the stranger in the mirror, a surge of what I can only describe as pure self-hatred ran through my body.

"I hate you, I hate you, I hate you!" I screamed at the teary-eyed reflection staring back at me.

I watched the pain darken my eyes as I felt the words jab like a knife; a feeling of worthlessness crept into every inch of my body. I was angry. I was tired of not being good enough. I was done competing with *everyone*. It seemed that no matter how hard I tried, no matter how hard I worked, it was never enough.

I was never enough.

Every day, I was trying so hard underneath my tough act—to win people's approval, to be loved, to feel like I had finally done enough to be worth something. There was nothing I could do to erase my flaws, but my achievements felt like a bandage I could put over them. As a result, I was constantly trying to achieve *more*. In high school, my classmates voted me "Most Likely to Succeed" and class president. If there was a group I could excel in, I was there. I was in a special honor student class and prided myself on being the best of the best.

But I knew I was running… from my hurt, from people, from rejection.

I was a different sort of addict. I kept medicating the pain I felt with accomplishments, but when it was just me, the fear and feelings of worthlessness always came rushing back.

I remember making a pact with myself as a young girl. "You're not pretty, so you're going to be smart," I promised. "You'll work harder than everyone else so people can see that you're worth something."

In my late teens, I found myself having a severe emotional breakdown from the intense stress I put on myself. When boys began to show an interest in me, that same insecurity led to heartbreak, and I hardened my heart more and more toward *the male species*.

Soon, I had developed a very unhealthy approach to life: *Hurt people, namely men, before they hurt me.*

I sat crying in an abortion clinic one day, making a decision I never imagined making in my wildest dreams. When I found out I was pregnant, the fear, guilt, and disappointment that welled up in me were unbearable. I had *plans*. I had *goals*. I *didn't* want to be a mother *ever*, let alone as a teenager.

The counselor told me that my decision would make everything better, that it would give me my old life back, that it was just an inconvenient blob of tissue—but it didn't, it didn't, and it wasn't!

Things got worse.

So much worse.

IT WAS ALL A LIE

That's when I realized I had been sold a lie. Actually, a pack of lies—lies about what it meant to be a woman, what it meant to be happy, and what it meant to be successful. Lies from our culture, from my teachers, and, worst of all, from myself…

But I couldn't lie anymore.

My excuses had been ripped away and everything I had spent years fighting for was suddenly laid bare before me in all of its brokenness.

I sat on my bed, wrecked, contemplating the two decisions that had been rolling around in my head for days….

I could kill myself.

Or I could pick myself up, dust myself off, and try to find the truth about happiness, about men and women, and about life.

ARE WE LEANING IN OR LEANING ON?

I was in Washington, D.C., for a political dinner a few years ago and there happened to be a large, very heated women's march going on at the same time. Women were crowding into the streets, shouting that they were *nasty* women and waving pro-abortion signs. Some even wore hats shaped like… well, vaginas. They were a sight to behold.

(*As a side note, if at any point in your life you end up with a vagina-shaped hat on your head, something has gone terribly wrong!*)

I couldn't help but reflect on my own journey out of the feminist movement and how far God had brought me from the broken, suicidal young girl who swore she would never get married or have children. I now walked hand-in-hand with my husband, who was and is one of the greatest joys in my life. I smiled up at him as I thought about my five other joys back home in Ohio—our children.

Praise God for the incredible work He has done in my life!

As my husband, Gary, and I walked to lunch during our stay in Washington, I passed three women who were a part of the protest. They wore shirts that read "NASTY WOMEN" in large letters.

I stopped for a moment, unable to resist starting a conversation with them. "Why do you want to call yourselves nasty women?" I asked.

Their answers were dripping with bitterness toward men—a sentiment I couldn't judge because I was once in their shoes. In fact, I have no doubt I would have been leading the way at that very march, proclaiming abortion and man-hating were the answers…

If not for the fact that those lies almost destroyed my life. *There, but for the grace of God…*

BUT WHAT'S TRULY NASTY…

After listening politely to them, I commented, "Some would say that demanding the right to take the lives of our own children, including fellow women, by the hundreds of thousands *is* a nasty business. What would you say to them?"

It must have struck a chord. The women stuttered to answer and almost seemed to soften before turning cold again. Then they claimed that birth control had decreased the abortion rate.

By a percentage or two, the margin of error? I thought.

I had to move on, but I knew our encounter was purposeful. The woman who was about thirty years younger than her leader looked to the older woman as if to ask the same question. Sadly, younger women seeking the approval of what they think are supposedly strong women are getting their answers from self-proclaimed nasty women. I was there. They aren't answers but distractions.

Less murder is still murder. The Guttmacher Institute reports, "In 2014, about half (51%) of abortion patients in the United States reported that they had used a contraceptive method in the month they became pregnant."[1] The simple truth is, no matter how many people believe or speak a lie, it doesn't make it any truer. It's easy to accept the messages we hear so often in the media as our truth, but we *have* to ask our own questions.

---

1. www.guttmacher.org/news-release/2018/about-half-us-abortion-patients-report-using-contraception-month-they-became.

Statistically, today women have more rights and freedoms than ever, but they are *less happy* than at any time in measured history.[2] Please don't misunderstand me; I am pro-women's right to equality. The feminist movement, which was once founded on seemingly good intentions, is no longer about equality in work, pay, or choices. It's about the choice to become "like men"—to discount the distinct DNA and masterminded purpose God has placed in each of us and demand the right to destroy another human being's life in the name of choice.

MEN AND WOMEN ARE EQUAL, BUT WE'RE NOT THE SAME, NOR WERE WE CREATED TO BE.

We've confused *equality* with being the *same*. Men and women are equal, but *we're not the same*, nor were we created to be.

So, let me ask you...

+ Have women truly *leaned in* and advanced in life, or have we just stopped leaning on the right source and lost all meaning for life in the process?

+ In the pursuit of becoming the same, have we lost what truly made us shine?

+ Is it possible to be accomplished, intelligent, impactful, and be a woman who's *not* nasty?

+ Do women have to become nasty to get what we want? And wouldn't that make our attitudes just as abhorrent as those we supposedly perceive in men and criticize?

+ Is it possible for men and women to get along?

+ Is motherhood a demeaning position in life, to be prioritized as the least impactful calling and vocation? Do we no longer believe "the hand that rocks the cradle is the hand that rules the world"?

---

2. Arianna Huffington, "The Sad, Shocking Truth About How Women Are Feeling," November 17, 2011; www.huffpost.com/entry/the-sad-shocking-truth-ab_b_290021.

* Where are the men in all of this? Have they gone into hiding or taken on nastier roles to counter women?

Many years ago, two women forever changed the world when they went after a plan to better their lives. One chose to base that plan on God's design for her. The other listened to a different voice, a voice that subverted leadership and offered a plan that questioned God and rebelled against Him.

TWO WOMEN FOREVER CHANGED THE WORLD. ONE LISTENED TO THE ENEMY, WHILE THE OTHER LISTENED TO GOD.

The choices of these two women affected eternity.

At the time, when the world was new, Eve must have believed that the voice she heard would bring her and her children a better future. Disguised as a snake, crafty Satan told her that if she ate from the forbidden tree *"your eyes will be opened, and you will be like God, knowing good and evil"* (Genesis 3:5). Eve had no idea what evil was, but it sounded good at the time. The results were painful—and nasty.

The other woman was Mary, who let her life be used by God for His glory. Told by an angel that she would bear the Son of God, she said, *"Behold, I am the servant of the Lord; let it be to me according to your word"* (Luke 1:38 ESV). Her desire to follow God and "lean on" His everlasting arms changed her life, her family, and the world forever.

One woman was deceived by the enemy, and her decision changed both the spiritual and physical realms. The other woman listened to God's messenger and changed both realms for His glory. She brought forth life!

As men and women, we have been given the spiritual capacity to impact and shape not only our own lives, but also the lives of other eternal beings. Our choices will ring throughout eternity. Will we live in pursuit of self-will… or God's will?

2

TIME FOR A NEW MOVEMENT

To truly understand what is happening in our culture today, we must first understand that the feminist movement is simply a *response* to the last movement that wreaked havoc on our country—one that specifically took a toll on women and the family. You could call it *a men's movement*, but I prefer to refer to it as *the John Wayne era*. You might know it best from the old 1950s movies where the leading man smacks the woman, then turns and kisses her.

In *The Quiet Man* (1952), John Wayne drags a "rebellious" Maureen O'Hara along the ground through sheep dung, followed by a crowd of amused villagers, while bright, lively music plays in the background. In *The Conqueror* (1956), he strikes Susan Hayward before kissing her. Of course, other actors portrayed men behaving badly on the big screen, too, like Robert Mitchum in *Angel Face* (1953) and Ronald Reagan in *The Killers* (1964). Men often slapped "hysterical" women to "calm them down" or because "they deserved it," sometimes to accompanying laugh tracks.

Images of men leaving their families and their marriages for younger women became a way of life on the big screen during the sixties sexual revolution. *That* was the picture of masculinity portrayed to many young boys in the mid-twentieth century.

MEN WERE MACHO; WOMEN PERFORMED

Men were culturally encouraged to be unfeeling, tough, often blunt, demanding, and even mean. Emotions were labeled as weakness. In order for many men to maintain their images of power and authority, to appear to be trendy or mainstream, they abused their positions as heads of their households instead of laying down their lives for their wives. (See Ephesians 5:25.) A movement of sexual liberation swept the nation through the new world of media and caused more abuse, more pain, and separation between men and women. Women strived to look good and *perform* to be worth something, competing with images in movies and magazines, often only to be hurt or rejected by men.

Women were not only belittled, excluded, and dishonored, but this movement hurt everyone involved—men, women, families, and especially children.

The John Wayne era failed our country and now another movement turns the tables with equal destruction. "Women Are the Future," according to the shirt one woman was wearing as I passed her in the airport.

Are we still missing it so greatly? Have we learned nothing from the past?

NOBODY WINS WHEN ONE GENDER BELITTLES, DOMINATES, OR CHEAPENS THE OTHER.

Nobody wins when one gender belittles, dominates, or cheapens the other. Families suffer. Society suffers. The abusers *and* the victims suffer.

When I was growing up, my mom, with all her great southern wisdom, always told me, "Two wrongs don't make a right." In other words, just because someone did something wrong to you, that doesn't mean it's okay for you to do something wrong back to them.

More hate is never the answer.

Nasty gets us nowhere!

NO WORDS OF LOVE

Gary's father grew up in the John Wayne era. He was a very hardened, cynical man, until he gave his life to God and was saved at the age of eighty. Gary never heard his father tell his mother he loved her *even once* while he was growing up. In fact, Gary's father never told *him* that he loved him either.

But when Gary's father was saved after eight decades of life, God did an amazing work in his heart, and he became a completely different man. My Navy veteran father-in-law, Thomas Keesee, would cry almost every time we came to see him, gushing about how proud he was of Gary. You couldn't talk to him without hearing him express how much he loved you.

"I've wasted my life," he told Gary one day. He was a successful businessman who started his own company—a company that lives on today—but that didn't matter to him anymore. He realized he had hardened his heart to what really mattered. Now his eyes were open… but he was out of time. Tom died peacefully at home, three years after being saved.

**WHEN PEOPLE HARDEN THEIR HEARTS,
THEY TRADE TRUE HAPPINESS FOR THE WORLD'S COUNTERFEIT AGENDA.**

Today, I see so many women who speak bitter, angry words, particularly when talking about men, and I can't help but wonder if they, too, will look back on their lives with regret, realizing they hardened their hearts and traded true happiness for the world's counterfeit agenda. Speaking from personal experience, it's an empty, broken path that does *not* lead to happiness!

JUSTICE... OR GETTING EVEN?

We have come such a long way since the John Wayne era, but many women still cling to the idea of *getting even*. The feminist movement has done its best to turn the tables on men. At its core, it's not about making things right; it's about getting *more* than justice—about women winning and men losing. Maybe that's not how it is for everyone, but unfortunately, that is the case for many. Today, we are seeing man-hating, belittlement toward men and an *anything you can do, I can do better* mindset running rampant. The teasing song by Irving Berlin has been turned into a thrown gauntlet or declaration of war.

I'm reminded of my mother's words: "Two wrongs *don't* make a right."

Galatians 5:15 says, "*If you bite and devour each other, watch out or you will be destroyed by each other.*"

We *all* lose when we tear each other down. The way the family goes is the way the nation goes—and the family unit doesn't work when we demean a *crucial* part of it.

Too often, men and women look at each other like opposing paddlers in a canoe race, both struggling to take the lead on a river only wide enough for one canoe. In reality, we are more like two paddlers racing in the same canoe. When one knocks the other out with their paddle, the canoe is likely to capsize.

MARRIAGE ISN'T ALWAYS EASY

My husband and I are very different, both in our natural roles as man and woman and in our personalities. I am *Mrs. Can Do, Sign Us Up for Everything…Our Flight Leaves in Five Minutes, We Still Have Time for Breakfast…Let's Talk About This for Three Hours…Life of the Party…I Haven't Slept in Three Days, But I Still Have Enough Energy to Shop at Marshall's…* Ha!

My husband is *Mr. Steady Plodder…I'd Rather Be in a Cabin in the Woods Than at a Party…Talking for Three Hours Straight Sounds Like a Nightmare…Let's Finish the Last Thing We Signed Up for Before We Sign Up for Something Else…Drenda, Didn't You Already Buy Three Bedazzled Plungers From HomeGoods?…* Ha!

Okay, that might be a little exaggerated, but sometimes, it really *does* feel like we are that different. And for the record, I have never bought a bedazzled plunger… but if I ever find one for sale, you bet I'd probably buy a couple.

My point is, when Gary and I were immature in our marriage, we attacked each other for the things we did differently and called out each other's weaknesses. We weren't complementing each other; we were competing with each other.

Today, after thirty-eight years of marriage, we know that what makes us different is what makes us *stronger* together. Our differences protect each other. As Proverbs 10:12 (ESV) says, *"Hatred stirs up strife, but love covers all offenses."*

WHEN WE WORK TOGETHER, THERE'S NOTHING THAT CAN STOP US.

Gary and I have also learned that we are in this together, whether we like it or not. Where one person goes, the other goes. When I tear down my husband, I tear down myself and our family. We are two canoeists in the same boat; if we don't agree on a direction, we're likely to end up spinning in circles and going nowhere. When we work together, there's nothing that can stop us. We are faster, more resilient, and stronger. People have actually called us a power couple. When men and women work together, they succeed together.

That's why a *men's* movement or a *women's* movement won't fix the problems in our culture. Neither one will make us happier, make our families stronger, or make us feel more fulfilled in life.

That's why even though women have gained more choices, rights, and opportunities since the John Wayne era, they are less happy than ever.

MEN ARE FIGHTING BACK

And that's why a lot of good men today are in hiding and others have started a war of their own against women in a backlash.

In an opinion piece for *Observer*, Andrea Tantaros wrote:

MIA: Men.

Feminism told them we didn't need them. Then we were told to emulate them. On top of it all, we've emasculated them, and now men are fighting back… quietly. American society has become increasingly anti-male. Men are sensing the backlash and are consciously and unconsciously going "on strike." *Breitbart* has dubbed this "equal but separate misery" between the sexes a "sexodus" where men are giving up on women altogether and stepping back from society. Statistics are showing that men are increasingly choosing not to get married….

One man commented[,] "Marriage is dead. Divorce means you are screwed for life. Women have given up on monogamy, which makes them uninteresting to us for any serious relationship or raising a family." Maureen Dowd once famously asked, "Are men necessary?" Now it's the men asking that about women—and, more importantly, about commitment. This isn't political, this is critical. It's time for both genders [to] admit we need each other, start treating each other with respect and concede that we're equal, but equal doesn't mean the same and embrace the differences in our wiring.[3]

On our mission to love and be loved, we have pushed ourselves *further* away from our goals.

WOMEN VS. WOMEN

MOTHERHOOD, THE FAMILY UNIT,
AND MARRIAGE HAVE TAKEN BIG HITS.

There has already been too much collateral damage in this gender war. Motherhood, the family unit, and marriage have taken big hits and have simply been shoved into the front lines as ammunition in the battle. And the attacks aren't just between men and women. Women have been pitted against each other, too—working moms versus stay-at-home moms,

---

3. Andrea Tantaros, "Five Ways Feminism Has Made Women Miserable: If we want a return to romance, we've got to start empowering men instead of emasculating them," *Observer*, May 3, 2016; observer.com/2016/05/five-ways-feminism-has-made-women-miserable.

married women versus single women, moms versus women without children, pro-choice versus pro-life... and the list goes on.

A Volkswagen commercial was recently banned in the United Kingdom for promoting gender stereotypes. Its offense? It showed a woman sitting next to a stroller.[4]

In an interview with singer Taylor Swift, a German interviewer was scolded after noting she was turning thirty and wondering "if she would like to be a mother someday." Swift refused to answer the question, noting, "I don't really think men are asked that question when they turn 30."[5]

Women, who were once one of the greatest cheerleaders for family, now march for the right to kill their own children inside the womb. According to the World Health Organization (WHO), there are around forty to fifty million abortions in the world every year. That's roughly five times the number of Jewish victims experts say were killed in the Holocaust—and it's happening year in, year out, right under our noses. What a plan from Satan!

When did being a mother become a shameful thing? When did demanding our own needs and "rights" become more important than standing for the defenseless and protecting our children, not to mention the women's rights of the little females in the womb?

MOTHERHOOD HAS BECOME A TABOO, TOUCHY TOPIC, TREATED MORE LIKE AN INSULT THAN THE POSITION OF HONOR GOD CREATED IT TO BE.

Motherhood has become a taboo, touchy topic, treated more like an insult today than the position of honor God created it to be. Satan loves to pit men and women against each other to destroy the very things that God

4. Rob Picheta, "Volkswagen and Philadelphia cream cheese ads banned over gender stereotypes," CNN Business, August 14, 2019; www.cnn.com/2019/08/14/media/uk-adverts-banned-gender-stereotypes-scli-gbr-intl/index.html.
5. Hayley FitzPatrick, "Taylor Swift shuts down interviewer when asked about wanting kids: Men aren't "asked that question," Good Morning America, May 28, 2019; www.goodmorningamerica.com/culture/story/taylor-swift-shuts-interviewer-asked-wanting-kids-men-63319368.

created to be sacred. This may be one of the sneakiest and costliest attacks of all.

WHEN A HAND UP HURTS

Even efforts to help marginalized women through economic develop-ment opportunities can backfire, as it did in Uganda:

> Traditional masculinities, hinged on men's ability to protect, pro-vide and rule, have been destabilised. One of the clear outcomes of this loss is an increase in violence. Gender-based violence was noted as a deterrent to women's political participation. Although some respondents indicated that the level of gender-based violence had gone down, the larger majority indicated that violence still persisted and that it impeded women's political participation.... Violence seems to be one of the mechanisms through which patri-archy is reinventing itself to subordinate women in a situation where the majority of men have clearly lost their dominant posi-tion in the household economy.[6]

Ugandan media is filled with stories about men making women do all the work, taking all their money to spend on themselves, and cheating on their wives or girlfriends. One man told a reporter:

> "This girlfriend of mine thinks I'm stupid, but I'm biding my time.... One night I spent 200,000 shillings on her and her friends and she gratefully told me that now she knows how much 'I love her'. Just wait until the ring is on her finger. I'm going to leave her in the house to take care of the children and enjoy my other women. That is how women deserve to be treated."[7]

By focusing solely on women's empowerment, many initiatives fail to bring lasting change because they inadvertently excuse or alienate men

6. Josephine Ahikire, Aramanzan Madanda, and Christine Ampaire, "Post-war economic opportunities in northern Uganda: Implications for women's empowerment and political participation," July 2012, International Alert/ Eastern Africa Sub-Regional Support Initiative for the Advancement of Women (EASSI); www.international-alert.org/sites/default/files/publications/201209WomenEconOppsUganda-EN.pdf.
7. Lindsey Kukunda, "Why Ugandan men suck!," Kampala Dispatch, November 25, 2016; dispatch.ug/2016/11/25/why-ugandan-men-suck.

from responsibility or obligation and essentially undermine masculine identity.

Women and men both succeed when they're working together. We *need* each other.

> *So God created mankind in his own image, in the image of God he created them; male and female he created them.* (Genesis 1:27)

WE REFLECT THE FULLNESS OF GOD

Together, we reflect the fullness of God. Even as women are economically empowered and society advances, it is not fully sustainable unless men are also included. As women take their place at the table alongside men in the ranks of every part of society, from leadership to labor to ministry, we will see more of the fullness of the kingdom of God on earth.

Jesus taught us, *"If a house is divided against itself, that house cannot stand"* (Mark 3:25).

Satan has been using bitterness, unforgiveness, and strife to blind us to what has really been going on right in front of our eyes—genocide, the destruction of marriage, suicide, families split apart… all-time highs for depression, anxiety, abortion, drug abuse, immorality, and loneliness, and all-time lows for successful marriages, happiness, couples getting married, men leading their families, and more.

Nasty gets us nowhere! Neither women nor men win at that game.

It's time to throw out the culture's *every man for himself* rule book and go back to the original guide. It's time to put aside men's movements and women's movements to end the destruction caused by gender wars. What we need is *a forgiveness and restoration* movement. We need to come together, build each other up, and speak to the strengths of each other's gender. We need a movement of *complementing* each other instead of *competing* with each other.

It's time for a movement toward unity and re-establishing God's design for life—that's the only way we can *all* succeed.

3

THE NASTY SHIFT

It seems today that men and women are more lost than ever. We've seen a dramatic shift away from the principles that once were the cornerstone of family life, marriage, and relationships. With technology, we have the world at our fingertips, and yet happiness has never seemed further from our grasps. As we've gained more independence and freedom, we've become more discontent.

So, when there are issues, who's the problem? Men or women?

Listening to the voices of anger and aggression today, it's hard to tell where the blame lies, but we know the tug-of-war between us started somewhere. And obviously blaming one another in anger isn't solving the problem; it's only making it louder and uglier.

OBVIOUSLY BLAMING ONE ANOTHER IN ANGER ISN'T SOLVING THE PROBLEM;
IT'S ONLY MAKING IT LOUDER AND UGLIER.

Women's boutiques are filled with shirts, aprons, and kitchen towels extolling the love of wine, chocolate, and dogs over the love of men. It doesn't sound like a recipe for happiness.

Yet a 2011 survey of 2,000 dog owners in the United Kingdom found that among women, almost one in five or 18 percent say they speak to their dog more often than to their partner.[8] Among U.S. dog owners of both sexes, 52 percent in a 2019 survey "admitted to kissing their dog more than their partner," and 52 percent said "they prefer to sleep in bed with their dog over their partner."[9]

A pet can be a joy and provide a little companionship, but it's not the same as a relationship with another person. No matter how fond we are of them, no dog, cat, or any other animal can offer the true love that we can receive from a human being.

When God created women, He said, *"It is not good for the man to be alone. I will make a helper suitable for him"* (Genesis 2:18). God created men and women to work as a team, whether at work, in marriage, or in the family!

Something must have shifted from His plan to the failures we see today. If we can discover the origin of this shift, perhaps we can understand the antidote.

Recently, I had to be away from Gary while ministering in Puerto Rico for a Happy Life kids' party. My women's ministry, Happy Life Women, hosted a neighborhood carnival event after hurricanes had ravaged the area. We secured enough Christmas presents to make several hundred children very happy and distributed them at the carnival.

Just before the carnival began, I received a call from our home alarm system that a fire was detected at our house. I knew Gary was supposed to be home, but the security company wasn't able to reach him. Then I remembered that he might be deer hunting so I told the company that they should dispatch the fire department.

Two fire trucks and an ambulance took off for our Georgian-style country home on sixty acres.

I was concerned and prayed, but I needed to focus on the children's party. Later, I received a text from Gary that all was well; he had simply

---

8. www.vettimes.co.uk/news/love-me-love-my-dog-say-surveys-doting-owners.
9. Kelli Bender, "Survey Finds Over Half of Dog Owners Kiss Their Pooches More Than Their Partners," *People*, July 5, 2019; people.com/pets/survey-dog-owners-kiss-dogs-more-than-partners.

started to cook his breakfast and left it to simmer while he stepped outside to hang up his deer. He didn't realize the simmer setting was hot enough to burn the food.

The kids' party was a hit, and I had the opportunity to bring the Sunday message at the local church we collaborated with to bless the kids. It was a great weekend and I couldn't wait to get home. I felt truly homesick. I had spent most of the last three months traveling and ministering; this was the last stop before Christmas. Our flight was delayed and every moment seemed to drag as I thought of the smell of home and the feel of my comfy bed. Mostly, though, I deeply missed my husband.

At 2:00 a.m., our flight finally took off! Home sweet home, here I come!

I arrived at 6:30 a.m. after a connection and a few hours of sleep. Gary picked me up and we were elated to see each other and get breakfast together. Although tired, with a new surge of energy, I began my overdue Christmas shopping. Christmas was only a week away! We kept going until we could go no more and finally arrived home at about 5:00 p.m.

Something was wrong.

The house smelled like smoke.

That was it! Gary's fire!

I had forgotten. Gary detailed again the story of how he wasn't gone long and just didn't think a low-simmering pan would start a fire so quickly. The house had a horrible scorched smell and I couldn't help but feel agitated about the near-disaster.

"I can't believe you almost caught our house on fire! I better not leave you home alone again," I teased. He was embarrassed, and I knew it, but I thought it was a good lesson to school him, my motherly punishment.

The rest of the evening, I searched for ways to get the smell out of our house. Several websites suggested boiling white vinegar with water, so that's what I did. The following morning, I did it again, but our house still reeked with that awful, smoky smell. Imagine the horrible smell of burnt popcorn, except it's in every room of your house.

Later, while I was getting my nails done, my nail technician asked if anything exciting had happened that week. I began to tell her about Gary's pan fire. (I don't make it a practice to share my husband's mistakes, but this was still very much on my mind.)

Fire!

Suddenly, I had an epiphany! *I* had left a pan of boiling vinegar on the stove! Almost two hours ago!

In panic, I started to hyperventilate as I told my nail tech what happened. She quickly wrapped up my session, and I took off in a mad dash to get home. I drove 75 mph with my flashers on, praying frantically and driving like a madwoman. I could just see the fire department at my house again for the second time in one week.

They may think we are arsonists trying to burn down our own house, I thought. *What if the house is really on fire? What if I've destroyed Christmas? We built that house from scratch with our family!*

I tried to pray instead of worry. A whirl of thoughts tried to capture me as I drove insanely. "Thank You, God, I will make it in time and our house will not be on fire!"

My goal was to get there not only before a fire started, but before the alarms sounded and the fire department was dispatched. I came flying into our driveway, ran into the hazy smoky kitchen leaving the door open, threw open a window, grabbed the charred pan off the stove, and quickly threw it out the window. It bounced off the hot tub cover and rolled down the yard. I ran around, opening the front door and holding my breath, hoping the alarm wouldn't go off.

Silence.

No alarm.

All was quiet except for the wind that whisked through the house. I had made it! No fire trucks. No paramedics. No damage.

Except the house smelled worse than ever.

Then it hit me: I had done the same thing Gary did. I almost burned the house down. I had shamed him a bit for something I myself was now guilty of.

I lay on the floor, out of breath and relieved. I was so happy I'd gotten there in time. Then I began to laugh and laugh, partly out of relief and partly because I deserved this.

When Gary got back from the office, we both had a very good laugh. He didn't shame me, but I could tell he was amused. I no longer wanted to tell the story about Gary's fire. I had my own story.

Our oldest daughter said, "I can't leave either of you alone! You two don't need a stove!"

Instead of shaming each other, Gary and I shared in a common mishap and because we both experienced the same feelings, we could laugh. We could feel one another's pain yet enjoy the humor in it. That's companionship. That's empathy. That's understanding.

Bear with each other and forgive one another if any of you has a grievance against someone. Forgive as the Lord forgave you.
(Colossians 3:13)

We often make the same mistakes and yet fail to help one another. We judge, blame, and find fault with the opposite sex, but we do the same things we complain about them doing. Rather than seeing ourselves clearly, we maximize their failures and minimize our own.

NOBODY IS PERFECT. REMEMBER, YOU MAKE MISTAKES TOO, SO GIVE SOME GRACE. FORGIVE QUICKLY AND LAUGH OFTEN.

Nobody is perfect. Remember, you make mistakes too, so respond to others with the same grace you would like them to extend to you. Forgive quickly and laugh often.

Isn't it always easier to blame someone else instead of looking at ourselves? Taking personal responsibility for our own contribution to the problem requires humility, but it's the key to resolution.

What if we worked on our own issues? Romans 2:3 says, "*So when you, a mere human being, pass judgment on them and yet do the same things, do you think you will escape God's judgment?*"

THE BLAME/SHAME GAME

The blaming and shaming between men and women started with the first man and woman, Adam and Eve. In a place of total bliss—better than Bora Bora or Hawaii—there was perfection in their surroundings. Eve was still not happy, even though she had everything—perfect love and a utopian garden. She also had a responsibility for her own choices—choices of either disobedience or godliness, for God gifted the first couple with free will.

There wasn't even a friend to compare her home, furnishings, or husband to and yet, somehow, Satan, the serpent, managed to talk Eve into feeling like there was more and God was holding out on her!

The serpent denied any negative outcomes for disobeying God; instead, he accused and blamed the Creator, saying:

"You will not surely die. For God knows that when you eat of it your eyes will be opened, and you will be like God, knowing good and evil."
(Genesis 3:4–5 ESV)

Eve believed the lie, and using her influence and place of adoration in Adam's life, she encouraged him to partake; choosing the rebellion-rooted fruit of disobedience, they ate from the Tree of the Knowledge of Good and Evil.

Together, they shared in the lie. It cost them everything! They turned from the beauty of God's design, creating conflict for themselves, their children, grandchildren, and all generations after them. A curse came on them not because of God or His plan, but because they took matters into their own hands.

I think it's worth reading this curse in Genesis 3:12–19:

The man said, "The woman you put here with me—she gave me some fruit from the tree, and I ate it." Then the LORD God said to the woman, "What is this you have done?" The woman said, "The serpent deceived me, and I ate." So the LORD God said to the serpent, "Because you have done this, cursed are you above all livestock and all wild animals! You will crawl on your belly and you will eat dust all the days of your life. And I will put enmity between you and the woman, and between your offspring and hers; he will crush your head, and you will strike his heel." To the woman he said, "I will make your pains in childbearing very severe; with painful labor you will give birth to children. Your desire will be for your husband, and he will rule over you." To Adam he said, "Because you listened to your wife and ate fruit from the tree about which I commanded you, 'You must not eat from it,' cursed is the ground because of you; through painful toil you will eat food from it all the days of your life. It will produce thorns and thistles for you, and you will eat the plants of the field. By the sweat of your brow you will eat your food until you return to the ground, since from it you were taken; for dust you are and to dust you will return."

Life was radically altered because of the curse. God said, *"Because you listened...."* It was Adam and Eve's choice to open themselves up to the curse, although they probably didn't know the ramifications of their decisions.

Originally, Adam and Eve had no shame and could freely know each other, walk together, work together, and have deep, meaningful companionship. There was no competition between them. They were both secure, experiencing love and loving one another. After their choice to disobey God, this fellowship and oneness was broken; they began to justify themselves and even accuse each other, following the serpent's example.

The same accusatory voice of Satan that caused their demise tempts us to shift the blame on one another. Instead of companionship and accomplishment among men and women, we often fight for our way and shame each other.

Interestingly, Adam blamed both God and Eve when God asked him why he ate. Adam said, "This woman *You* gave me told me to eat, and so I did."

I like to imagine God thinking, *If Eve told you to jump off a cliff, would you?* But I doubt that's where that phrase came from. Ha!

Eve followed Adam's example—remember that—and said, "The serpent told me to eat it."

Everyone is blaming someone else. But blaming others without taking personal inventory will only keep us in a state of brokenness and dysfunction, possibly nursing a victim mentality. We have *all* been hurt and bear the scars of living in an earth-cursed world with evil supernatural activity and spiritual strongholds.

WE CAN'T SUCCEED TOGETHER UNLESS WE SHED THE CLOAK OF THE CURSE AND LEARN TO FIGHT THE REAL SOURCE OF OUR CONFLICT AND STRUGGLE: THE ENEMY'S LIES.

We can't succeed together unless we shed the cloak of the curse and learn to fight the real source of our conflict and struggle: the enemy's lies.

THE ENEMY'S LIES

The curse that was set in motion must be dealt with or we can never be free or realize our design and destiny. The enemy is still accusing, blaming, and shaming women and men into believing lies about one another and about God.

God's plan of marriage has been questioned and attacked. Millennials are either delaying or denying marriage altogether. Abortion is the outcome of sex without family commitment. As a result, many nations such as Italy have fallen into a negative population growth; America is not too far behind, with the national rate of population growth at its lowest level since 1937.[10]

A nation is only as strong as its families.

After years of fighting for women's rights, equality in pay, and opportunities for women to compete in sports at all levels, the curse has come full circle as men denying their biological maleness compete and win in women's sports competitions, ruling over their biological female opponents and stripping them of reward.

---

10. William H. Frey, "US population growth hits 80-year low, capping off a year of demographic stagnation," Brookings Institution (www.brookings.edu/blog/the-avenue/2018/12/21/us-population-growth-hits-80-year-low-capping-off-a-year-of-demographic-stagnation).

Women are on the offensive as well. Taking advantage of modern statistics on date rape and sexual assault, they seek out successful men for consensual sex and then accuse them of rape or sexual harassment. They also attempt to control men through media messages and in the workplace, demanding rules against men that women themselves often don't play by. Men are certainly not innocent either, bent on getting even. Who needs women or marriage? They're *straight*, they say, but an anti-feminist movement of men proclaims they're *going their own way*. They state they're "protecting and preserving their own sovereignty above all else," and that means meeting their needs apart from women. They turn to perverse, self-focused ways to pleasure themselves, like sex robots and self-satisfaction.

It's all retribution for the sins committed against one another and many are guilty in this game.

Most recently, these themes have played out in uncorroborated accusations and the near-destruction of Supreme Court Justice Brett Kavanaugh during his confirmation hearings. It's become fair to accuse and blame without any evidence. We are told victims have a right to be believed, but when we rush to judgment because of someone's gender instead of evidence, we undermine true justice and make a mockery of real victims of crime or abuse. It becomes difficult to know what to believe about someone. Sabotage for political or financial gain has become a political weapon and women have their fingers on the trigger.

It's escalated to a war that's out of control.

The curse of Adam and Eve continues regardless of the fight because human effort alone always seems to backfire; it can't get the job done or undo what the curse did. A curse does not stop without someone who can break it. Women have tried through anger, rebellion, demands, protests, marches, media messages, and downright hatred of men... but none of that has worked.

Men rule over women and women try to control men because the curse is still at work in this world. But male domination, whether forceful or cajoling, hasn't made men any happier either. They try to escape their pain through gaming, hobbies, gambling, sports, porn, or affairs. Or they become consumed with trying to overcome the financial curse that disobedience and Satan brought into the world. He promised Adam and

Eve so much—"*You will be like God*" (Genesis 3:5)—but in the end, the ground produced thorns and thistles, and Adam survived only through his own painful toil and sweat. Debt now offers a seemingly easy way out of the pressure, but it has enslaved and destroyed countless families and marriages, breaking people's spirits as financial hopelessness consumes the dreams they once had.

Male or female, they will both be lied to over and over again, grappling at the next promise of freedom only to wind up empty-handed. It will result in abuse, manipulation, prostitution, abortions, rape, debt, sex trafficking, broken hearts, murder, addictions, and suicides—even among children.

Eve's desire was for Adam, but he ruled over her and the earth produced trouble for them both. Not much has changed.

If only there were a way to return to God's plan, a curse-breaker to allow us to escape from this cycle of destruction....

The good news is, there is!

A REDEEMING LOVE

There was a woman at a well in Samaria. (See John 4:7–42.) She had three strikes against her:

+ She was a woman in a male-dominated culture.
+ She was a Samaritan, the lowest economic and cultural group.
+ She had been married five times and was now living with a man who was not her husband.

Jesus approached this woman at the well and asked her for a drink of water. She was astonished since a Jewish rabbi would never speak to such a woman.

In the course of their conversation, Jesus told her about her past; in a direct word of knowledge, He read her mail. She was once again astonished that He knew about her five husbands and current live-in situation. She told Jesus, "*I can see that you are a prophet*" (John 4:19). Since He clearly was a prophet, she mentioned the different places where Jews and Samaritans worshiped, hoping He would shed some light on the matter. When Jesus answered her, she knew that the Messiah would eventually come and explain everything.

Jesus told her, "I am He."

What?

In John's gospel, the first person to whom Jesus revealed His identity as the Messiah was not one of his disciples, but rather this woman at a well who clearly lived with a disappointing past.

I believe this is precisely why Jesus shared this news with her. He knew her search for love with men had left her empty and unhappy. She was so elated that He valued her, speaking to her as a person of worth, that she left her water jar and ran back to town, telling anyone who would listen, *"Come, see a man who told me everything I ever did. Could this be the Messiah?"* (John 4:29).

It's interesting that Jesus confronted her with her problem, her wrongdoing, not to condemn her, but so that she might clearly see her need for Him—the Messiah, the curse-breaker. He spoke truth to her, not ignoring her sin, but bringing His love and the answer she so desperately needed to hear.

We don't know why this woman had five husbands. We don't even know her name—perhaps to spare her shame, or maybe because the story could carry my name, or the name of many others who could in some way relate to her. Jesus valued her and gave her victory over a past filled with hurt. Then He gave her a voice and vision for her life. Jesus modeled how we should treat the earth-cursed failings of life and how we can find vision again.

God loves women and men. He created marriage as a beautiful union between them and He sent His Son, Jesus, to break the curses that have plagued men and women, to restore His original vision for the relationship between them. Men and women both have a voice in the world, and we need to figure out how to shift our relationships to affirm what God says and how He says our relationships will work. We must shift from the darkness of the curse into the light of God's kingdom of hope and faith in one another.

WHAT ARE YOU LOOKING FOR?

Jesus taught us, *"Seek and you will find"* (Matthew 7:7). This spiritual principle applies to everything in our life, both good and bad.

When we believe something, we have a tendency to make it happen. If we believe men are the problem, then we will find supporting evidence to prove it. If we believe women are impossible to please, then we will be able to cite circumstances to back that up. If we believe marriage is a pain and divorce is inevitable, that will most likely become our experience.

OUR MINDSETS INFLUENCE THE WAY WE FILTER
OTHER PEOPLE'S WORDS AND ACTIONS. IF A CONFLICT HAS ARISEN,
STEP BACK AND EXAMINE YOUR FILTER.

Our mindsets influence the way we filter other people's words and actions. If a conflict has arisen, step back and examine your filter. Is a preconceived mindset affecting your ability to read the situation?

Obviously, with every endeavor, there are challenges and investments that must be made. However, we can't look at the cost alone without also recognizing the benefits and rewards or we will reject the idea altogether. That's the danger of the anti-marriage, pro-women/anti-men, or anti-women messaging of today. If we hear it long enough—which isn't hard to do thanks to daily media propaganda and messaging—we believe it. We buy into the remediation, creating false beliefs about the possibility of working and succeeding together or experiencing lasting relational commitment.

Without commitment, the benefits and joys of relationship with the opposite sex will fail. It was doomed to begin with because of wrong beliefs that the effort and risk weren't worth the return or benefit. That sly serpent Satan has been brainwashing the world ever since he first said, *"Did God really say…?"* (See Genesis 3:1.) We are witnessing a great delusion of lies and challenges against God's good plans for women and men.

So can we get along without getting nasty? This is the golden question!

Probably not, if you're trying to turn him or her into a dog that graduated from obedience school, or expect them to provide you with lifelong bliss. First, dogs are pets—and people are not pets. Second, there is no instant gratification in relationships, no quick fix or euphoric bliss every day. People don't do what you want all the time (neither do pets), but relationships done well, seasoned with age and maturity, satisfy the soul and offer companionship that is beyond any other, certainly more than any pet, bottle of wine, or slice of cheesecake.

Jesus told the woman at the well that He could give her a drink and she would never thirst again. For women and men to first get along, we must drink from this well of life-giving love. We can't give each other something we do not possess.

Only by breaking the curse can we find wholeness and happiness.

Years of working in business and ministry, and building a fulfilling marriage, have taught me practical, spiritual principles that will help men and women communicate better, understand each other better, work together, and, most importantly, honor one another.

We *can* break the curse off our relationship and truly succeed together. That was God's plan in the beginning, and it's still His plan for us today.

4

WHAT WERE YOU THINKING?

When Gary and I were first engaged, he took me dove hunting. Yes, I went from a feminist to trying to impress this man!

Now, for you to truly understand how out of my element I was, you have to know that I was a *city* girl from Georgia. I didn't grow up on a pecan farm or in some sparsely populated town out West. As a young girl, I thought hunting was the grossest, weirdest thing that one could do and my worst nightmare was marrying a boy from up North who was a hunter. In fact, when I was mad at my parents, I would threaten to marry a Northern boy and move. Ha!

Words have power, because that's exactly what happened.

I agreed to go hunting with Gary because it sounded fun and adventurous. I imagined this romantic hunting trip with us two prancing around the woods, like Tarzan and Jane, where I would get a perfect shot, and my fiancé would swoon at having such an incredible future wife… at which point, he would take me shopping.

Gary taught me how to shoot the gun and left me in position. When I saw a flock of birds and I pulled up and shot, Gary came over, laughing a bit at my attempt.

"What?" I asked, my ears still ringing from the gunshot.

"You're cute," he remarked with a coy smile. *Well, that's not quite what I was going for*, I thought, *but I'll take it!*

It turns out that I shot a bird all right, but it was a sparrow, not a dove. (Yes, I know, His eye is on the sparrow.) Gary hadn't given me any bird species lessons. It never occurred to Mr. Hunter that I didn't know the difference between a dove and a sparrow.

He went on to explain the differences. It was Greek to me. Why did anyone care about the differences? I guess they don't taste the same. Then Gary pulled up, casually shot a dove, and showed me the difference.

Warning: this story is about to get more graphic.

Shockingly, using his thumbs, Gary popped out the bird's breast and stuck it in the pocket of his hunter's jacket.

Gasp!

That was the day I decided not to be a hunter, but rather to be a gatherer—not of birds but of other things… you know, like things I find on sale at the grocery store.

When Gary and I first got married, that was the first time I really realized how different men and women are. Gary and I liked different things, but more importantly, we communicated and saw the world through totally different point of views.

In order for men and women to succeed together, we first have to understand that we *are* different, and we need to understand what *makes* us different. Men and women are not only physiologically very different, we are two separate, distinct creations of God. God made man from the dirt and woman from man. We are equal, but certainly not the same.

MEN AND WOMEN HAVE DIFFERENT STRENGTHS AND WEAKNESSES, BUT THAT MAKES US STRONGER WHEN WE WORK TOGETHER!

Men and women have different strengths and weaknesses, but that makes us powerful when we work together!

Then the LORD God formed a man from the dust of the ground and breathed into his nostrils the breath of life, and the man became a living being. (Genesis 2:7)

Then God took one of the man's ribs and fashioned a woman from it.

Upon seeing Eve, Adam said, *"This is now bone of my bones and flesh of my flesh; she shall be called 'woman,' for she was taken out of man"* (Genesis 2:23).

Someone once asked me, "Do you really believe that, Drenda?"

Yes, I do!

In many ways, we are the same, but in very significant ways, we are not alike at all. It's almost ludicrous that some women have spent their lives fighting to disprove this fact when it doesn't take a rocket scientist to see the undeniable truth. Men or women can try to imitate the other sex, but it's only imitation. Margarine is not butter, no matter what the packaging looks like, nor is burlap silk. Woman was formed from man for companionship with him; God created us to complement each other.

This isn't just proven in the Bible, it's proven in science, too—in human behavior, physiology, biology, and neurology, to name just a few fields. Men and women *are* different. Our DNA and origins tell the story. This is most certainly not an issue of capability or intelligence, but a difference in design.

There are general, overarching distinctions between men and women that are universally observed, studied, and recorded in every part of the world. Obviously, each of us is a product of not only God's design but also our environment, experiences, and personal choices. Yet environmental differences do not greatly change the tendencies of human nature and physiological makeup distinguishing us. The difference between our genders is a great strength when understood, honored, and utilized, whether in marriage, business, ministry, or culture.

WHERE ARE YOU FROM?

A well-known best-seller from the 1990s, written by John Gray, is titled *Men Are from Mars, Women Are from Venus.* But I think if men are from Mars, women are from another galaxy.

When Gary comes home after spending time fishing with a friend or our sons, my first questions are always the same: "How did it go? Did you have a nice time?"

IF MEN ARE FROM MARS, WOMEN ARE FROM ANOTHER GALAXY.

"Good!" my husband says, followed by a short description of the fish that were caught.

"That's awesome! What did you guys talk about?" I eagerly respond, ready to get to the good stuff.

My husband stares at me as blankly as if I've just asked him to recite the alphabet from Z to A.

"Nothing really," he says, still confused by the question.

"You were out there for four hours. You must have talked about something interesting!" I insist.

My husband does his best to recall the details I care about until I'm satisfied—meanwhile, I sit in wonder at how his brain works.

If my husband were telling the same story with the roles reversed, he would say the exact opposite about me. My attention to detail and my desire to fill him in on everything are overwhelming. When Gary asks me how a shopping trip with our daughters went, I tell him how our daughters are doing, what we talked about, the new shirt Amy wore, each piece of clothing I bought, the funny thing our waitress said, the delicious dessert we ordered… the list goes on. He may not want to hear it, but I can remember every detail that happened and everything that was said. *And* I'm more than happy to relive the whole day with him.

Now, after years of marriage, my wonderful husband pays extra attention to the details that he knows I'll be interested in when he's out. Meanwhile, I try to keep my stories to the headlines so I don't bore him. Ha!

Men and women approach life from differing perspectives. Men jump into life, learning as they experience, and *do* life. They learn through doing and find their expression outwardly seeking to explore and discover by going on adventures, conquering or building things, or, in Gary's case, hunting. I think of men as explorers or possibly pirates. This isn't to say that women are not adventurous or gung-ho about life, but usually, our adventures find meaning from those with whom we share them. We may sail the seas, but it's probably because we fell in love with a pirate and want his time and attention. (Just kidding, of course!)

A woman tends to be more contemplative and learns from her own reflections. She sees herself in relation to those around her; the experience itself is just the setting. Overall, she sees in detail, creates and admires beauty, and savors engaging in dialogue, even if it's only in her head. As they age, women are much more likely than men to talk aloud to themselves. Women process through communication. We want relationships and find meaning and direction in the context of reflecting off of others. Conversation is the key way we derive meaning from relationships—even if it's bossing ourselves around after our children move out!

Women are less likely to live in a state of continually taking on endeavors that are unsafe or risky in nature, since we not only crave love and relationship but also value security and safety. This isn't to say we can't be daring; we simply don't want to risk having someone we love get hurt or us not being able to fulfill the needs of those who depend on us emotionally. Think nurturer. Overall, it is much easier for women to engage in riskier behavior before motherhood.

Gary and I rode a motorcycle together in the early stages of our relationship nearly forty years ago. I had no worries about riding with him and saw it as alone time with a friend whom I wanted to know better relationally. I rode to connect with him more deeply. I enjoyed it, yes, but mostly because he was there. I would have just as easily gone sailing. Gary rode a motorcycle because he loved it and wanted to share his hobby with me.

Once we married and children entered the picture, I went into mother hen mode. I could not see myself taking the risk to ride a fast, Kawasaki 1000 "bike" with no real protection between me and the road. I really didn't want Gary to ride either. I viewed our responsibilities to our children as primary in comparison to the adventure of riding. Once our children were adults, I shifted back into allowing myself to enjoy a motorcycle journey with Gary and we've been on some pretty intense road trips and experiences together.

Why the change?

My desire to be with my husband on an adventure was once again my primary relational focus. My children were no longer depending on me.

Typically, the risk factor would not enter into a man's mind except if his wife planted it there. This *reward vs. risk vs. responsibility* reasoning is important in decision-making, which is why women are often credited with having wisdom that is not the same as a man's logical way of processing. In general, if men want to do something, they simply *do* it if it makes logical sense to them. They're inclined to just do it, often without regard to the overarching impact it may have on others.

Women more typically weigh the outcome over the risk, not based on logic but rather on innate wisdom gained from a broader perspective. Whether you call it a woman's intuition or a sixth sense, a woman's contemplative nature helps her to *feel* her way through situations and decisions. She won't primarily lean on logic, but rather on how she feels intuitively and relationally about the matter. Some of these realities have been attributed to brain differences. It's a part of God's created design.

For many business decisions that Gary and I faced through the years, whether in the companies we built or in our ministry, I was key in either warning or encouraging him on whether we should take the leap. If I knew something could advance us and I had the inner sense that it would be good for our family, I often pushed Gary way past his comfort zone to *go for it*. Why? Because I believed in him and wanted great things for us as a family. Major decisions we made as a couple that ultimately promoted us came about through heart-to-heart talks, sometimes with tears and sacrifices we made together.

Women like to talk through the details and see the broader picture, then make a decision after weighing every possibility. Probably the best example of this tendency is the way most women approach shopping. Generally speaking, females want to view many options and touch, feel, and see before making a purchase. If we need a blue shirt, we may examine four options at different stores. We may end up not only purchasing a blue shirt or two, but we might also accumulate other items in our shopping cart as we recall a multitude of upcoming needs or events. We multitask and think in detail. Not only do we think about the blue shirt, but also we consider the needs of our children, husband, and perhaps our best friend, the church, and the next birthday.

Typically, a man will simply focus on one thing, go into a store, and just buy a blue shirt—probably the first one in the right size that looks comfortable. To him, it's blue; to you, it's teal blue. Again, I'm generalizing a bit about man's ability to compartmentalize and focus like a laser beam, mission accomplished. Women see in many details and multitask, which we often think is the right way to do things. We can be wiser for it, but this way of thinking can also distract us.

In the past, I could easily turn this ability into a controlling or uppity, *I am smarter than you* attitude because I could recall many details about varying events at lightning speed. My mouth could fire them off like a machine gun.

But neither women nor men are superior to the other; we are just different in our approaches and processing. It's a man's innate strength to stay focused on one pursuit at a time. It's a woman's innate strength to weigh all factors before making a decision.

DEALING WITH HURT

A woman's ability to remember and think in detail can become a weakness if she allows feelings to rule her relationships, especially if she tends to nurse wounds or disappointments. Because women see details and have the memory of an elephant—specifically when it comes to relationships—we also tend to hold on to hurts if we allow ourselves to do that. We can belabor an issue and rehearse it until it becomes destructive. Men typically will drop an issue and can't understand why we don't do that. They can fight one day—even trading punches—and be all buddy-buddy the next day, the battle forgotten. Men have the ability to see problems externally and determine solutions, whereas women internalize issues and sometimes take them personally.

Hurts are a place where this difference is glaring.

In my years of counseling couples, I have often had men say to me, "Why can't she just forgive me and move on?" For him, it's an instant, logical decision; for her, it's a breach of conduct requiring time and rebuilt trust to move forward. Conversely, when women err or are unfaithful, once the man decides to forgive, it's typically done. He won't bring it up again...but she may! She wants to understand and perhaps even justify the breakdown, and wants him to as well. Women process forgiveness through repeated conversations and working through failures and mistakes, even their own.

WOMEN PROCESS FORGIVENESS THROUGH REPEATED CONVERSATIONS
AND WORKING THROUGH FAILURES AND MISTAKES, EVEN THEIR OWN.

To a man, the woman is obsessing over a problem and just needs to let it go. However, this is a woman's way of working through an issue so that she *can* let go. She needs to talk about it: why it happened, the circumstances surrounding it, her feelings, his feelings—everything.

Sexual desire works the same way for her. It grows over a period of time through multiple conversations and time spent together to build a close, loving relationship.

If couples don't meet in the middle and understand that both of their approaches are needed, to both invest by talking through and, yes, eventually let go by moving on, then there isn't a strong future for their love.

COMMUNICATION IN THE WORKPLACE

These factors enter the workplace as well. Women introduce more detail in meetings and want to discuss various perspectives that are not simply based on logical observations. The relational aspect of women and the logical, factual approach of men can be a great asset in tandem decision-making, but if inner-office relationships sour, it can also be very divisive.

Recognizing and listening to both perspectives in the workplace gives a fuller picture of the options.

It's important that men and women respect and utilize their differing perspectives or the success of an organization will suffer. And because women can read women better than men can, challenges become intense when two women enter the picture, whether in the boardroom or in the home between a mother and a daughter. Conflicts between women who may confide in a male to reaffirm their opinion or a perceived offense are all too common. Women can read more into a situation, worry about outcomes, or not trust a female coworker and then confide in another coworker to find agreement, especially if they perceive a threat. These are dynamics that play out daily in male/female relationships.

THE DIFFERENCE IN OUR BRAINS

The differences between men and women are not just innate; our brains are dissimilar in many ways. We are wired differently. The book *Results at the Top: Using Gender Intelligence to Create Breakthrough Growth* by Barbara Annis and Richard Nesbitt[11] explores scientific information about the male and female brains that's fascinating. I like the term *gender intelligence*. It sounds cool.

The book is written primarily for men, to show them how organizational performance is better with women. The authors say there's "a virtually universal relationship between the presence of women on boards and in senior management teams and improved corporate performance."[12]

In a podcast with marketing consultant Roger Dooley, Annis notes that when talking about gender differences in the way men and women think, there's "a bell curve," but 80 percent of us "fall into these tendencies."[13]

The hippocampus—the region of the brain associated primarily with memory—is larger in women, so it makes sense why women can remember details so well. Women also have a larger prefrontal cortex, which helps them to consider consequences, control impulses, and plan for the future.

---

11. Barbara Annis, Richard Nesbitt, *Results at the Top: Using Gender Intelligence to Create Breakthrough Growth* (Hoboken, NJ: John Wiley & Sons, Inc., 2017).
12. Ibid.
13. Roger Dooley, "Breakthrough Growth Using Gender Intelligence," *Brainfluence Podcast*, July 6, 2017 (www.rogerdooley.com/gender-intelligence).

A girl's prefrontal cortex develops earlier in childhood, giving her an advantage for memorization in classroom settings. This accounts for why boys do not respond as well to such learning methods and why girls achieve at higher levels early on. Boys are more likely to be treated for attention deficit hyperactivity disorder and medicated to basically coerce them to conform to standards that favor girls' brains. This leads to a life of critiquing, demoralizing, and emasculating the God-designed nature of males.

Another brain difference in men is that they have a much larger amygdala, which is utilized in threatening situations to react aggressively in the need to protect or defend. Women store more memory and detail (think gatherer), while men focus on immediate threats and respond with the power to eliminate danger (think defender).

Our Creator gave men both the physical strength and the brains, if you will, to react as protectors. God gave women the power to navigate through their memory banks to find wise solutions. When we combine these strengths, we are unstoppable! But when we become divided and focus on our differences, the results can be emotionally, physically, and relationally unhealthy.

According to *Stanford Medicine*:

Women are twice as likely as men to experience clinical depression in their lifetimes; likewise for post-traumatic stress disorder. Men are twice as likely to become alcoholic or drug-dependent, and 40 percent more likely to develop schizophrenia. Boys' dyslexia rate is perhaps 10 times that of girls, and they're four or five times as likely to get a diagnosis of autism spectrum disorder.... Why are men's and women's brains different? One big reason is that, for much of their lifetimes, women and men have different fuel additives running through their tanks: the sex-steroid hormones.... Every cell in a man's body (including his brain) has a slightly different set of functioning sex-chromosome genes from those operating in a woman's....[14]

---

14. Bruce Goldman, "Two minds: The cognitive differences between men and women," *Stanford Medicine* magazine, Spring 2017 (stanmed.stanford.edu/2017spring/how-mens-and-womens-brains-are-different.html).

Not only do women have larger prefrontal cortexes, but also we have larger anterior cortexes. As a consequence, worry and anxiety are associated with women more than with men. So when we traditionally say God created men to bear the stress and pressure of going out, conquering, and providing for the family, our brain function backs up scriptural models and human nature itself. Women *can* do anything, *but* our brains affirm our strength to store detailed memory, which helps us nurture; our response to too much stress is emotional sadness, accounting for women experiencing twice as much depression as men and almost four times the usage of antidepressants.

> Women, it's known, retain stronger, more vivid memories of emotional events than men do. They recall emotional memories more quickly, and the ones they recall are richer and more intense. If, as is likely, the amygdala figures into depression or anxiety, any failure to separately analyze men's and women's brains to understand their different susceptibilities to either syndrome would be as self-defeating as not knowing left from right. [15]

DIFFERENCES AS CHILDREN

Human behavioral differences are significant between men and women; they can even be observed in infants. Baby girls tend to study faces, whereas baby boys are more preoccupied with things or objects. These differences become more pronounced over time. The *Stanford Medicine* article quotes Dr. Diane Halpern, past president of the American Psychological Association:

> There was too much data pointing to the biological basis of sex-based cognitive differences to ignore, Halpern says. For one thing, the animal-research findings resonated with sex-based differences ascribed to people. These findings continue to accrue. In a study of 34 rhesus monkeys, for example, males strongly preferred toys with wheels over plush toys, whereas females found plush toys likable. It would be tough to argue that the monkeys' parents bought them sex-typed toys or that simian society encourages its male offspring

---

15. Ibid.

to play more with trucks. A much more recent study established that boys and girls 9 to 17 months old—an age when children show few if any signs of recognizing either their own or other children's sex—nonetheless show marked differences in their preference for stereotypically male versus stereotypically female toys.[16]

HARDWIRED FOR SUCCESS

Halpern and others have found many human behavioral differences.

"These findings have all been replicated," she says. Women excel in several measures of verbal ability—pretty much all of them, except for verbal analogies. Women's reading comprehension and writing ability consistently exceed that of men, on average. They outperform men in tests of fine-motor coordination and perceptual speed. They're more adept at retrieving information from long-term memory. Men, on average, can more easily juggle items in working memory. They have superior visuospatial skills: They're better at visualizing what happens when a complicated two- or three-dimensional shape is rotated in space, at correctly determining angles from the horizontal, at tracking moving objects and at aiming projectiles.[17]

Men's brain activity looks different from women's even when men are resting. Men tend to disengage, unwind, and power off. Women, on the other hand, want to talk about the events of the day in order to process them. These are completely different approaches to relaxation! If he wants to disconnect and she wants to talk, how do you navigate these idiosyncrasies? Understanding that they exist is the first step.

Women will tend to want to interact with colleagues after a stressful meeting or interact with family, friends, and relatives at the end of a busy day. These activities help women produce oxytocin, increase relaxation, and relieve stress, which in itself produces even more oxytocin, a critical stress-reducing hormone.[18]

16. Ibid.
17. Ibid.
18. Annis and Nesbitt, *Results at the Top: Using Gender Intelligence to Create Breakthrough Growth.*

Men want to give their brains time to unwind and decide what to do next rather than communicate, or even think. In fact, when a man is relaxing, a woman might ask him, "What are you thinking?" When he says, "Nothing," she has a hard time believing him. But it's true—he's literally just zoned out.

> After a long or stressful meeting or at the end of a busy day, men tend to want to shut down and drift off—close off the world for a little while. Men tend to retreat and seek solitude or engage in some low-involvement activity such as watching the news or sports, or working on a small project. It's a natural tendency in a man to "turn off" in order to replenish testosterone, and that relieves his stress, relaxes, and reenergizes him.[19]

I have had to remind myself through the years to give Gary some solitary quiet time. Whether he takes a walk in the woods, a power nap, or a jog, he has to let his mind disengage from fight mode to rest. If I engage him with my tasks or issues of the day, he goes into problem-solving mode. I didn't realize I was tasking him to work; I simply saw it as us unwinding because that's what it is for me.

Men's heart rates tend to escalate when they talk, whereas women's rates tend to fall. Women usually find conversing both comforting and relational; for men, it seems like work. If a man rests first and has some power-down time, he is recharged and better able to listen.

I've learned to not babble like a chatty schoolgirl about things that Gary is likely to find meaningless—why someone's outfit was *clearly* out of place, for instance. I don't need to rehash every thought and event of the day, even if I'm tempted to do so. I am better off saving that for female friends or prayer. (I do hope *God* doesn't get tired of my babbling!)

Males largely want to hear the headlines and *do* things with women instead of hearing an excess amount of information from them. At some point, a man's brain will disengage if a woman tries to overwork it. There's a time for everything. "Silence is golden" most certainly was written by a man.

---

19. Ibid.

EVERYONE'S FAVORITE TOPIC: HORMONES

Obviously, men and women have differing levels of hormones, which affect brain activity, development, needs, and responses to one another. How do men press through hardships to succeed and perform heroic feats? Testosterone is linked to a man's competitive edge and ability to bounce back, fight the day-to-day pressures, and recover from trauma.

> Normal levels of testosterone are linked to feelings of success in men. When men face difficulty or failure, their testosterone levels will begin to drop and they'll experience lowered spirits or even feel depressed until their levels are replenished.[20]

Testosterone is replenished in men through rest and some solitude.

Another hormone, oxytocin, helps men and women bond, and both sexes release it in a trusting relationship where safety, security, and intimacy are experienced. Oxytocin can trick our brains into thinking we are in love early in a relationship when we're merely infatuated. It reduces blood pressure in both males and females and helps diminish anxiety and fear. While it can help married couples grow closer, it can also reduce inhibitions between coworkers. That's why spending inordinate amounts of time with a coworker, especially casually outside of working hours, can lead to sexual temptation. Reserve that time for your spouse, and let the oxytocin build.

In both men and women, our hormonal makeup affects just about everything.

I joke that there are Three Ps in life during which men need to be extremely understanding with women: premenstrual syndrome or PMS; pregnancy; and pre- and post-menopause. These are times when a female's hormones are fluctuating and flipping around like flapjacks.

We women also need to give ourselves some grace in these times. I have had to tell myself, "This too shall pass. This isn't really how you feel. Set your feelings on the shelf and revisit them next week." (But, guys, don't say anything like this to a woman! She will *not* appreciate it.)

---

20. Ibid.

Life is full of stressors. All of us, men and women, need understanding and cooperation to help each other through the highs, lows, and difficulties. Women's stress-inducing cortisol levels tend to be two to four times higher than a man's, in part because of brain differences. Women are not wired to handle a lot of traumatic stress.

Oxytocin-producing activities in women work to lower cortisol levels and reduce stress. But when women aren't able to collaborate at work, or there's not enough time to attend to personal life events and needs, their stress and anxiety will increase beyond their ability to relax and collect themselves. That increase in stress brought on by the rush of cortisol stimulates the production of testosterone in women's systems and inhibits their ability to produce oxytocin, thereby perpetuating the stress cycle.[21]

Women process stress and recover from its effects with someone to help them, to share their feelings, to know that they are understood—someone *gets* them. They're not alone. And the truth is, we are not!

Although a man can work to understand and be that someone for his wife, she should also remember that he can't possibly meet all her needs. That's one of the reasons a strong spiritual relationship with God will give us the comfort and calm we seek. Prayer and meditation on God's promises create rest and restore the soul, and He is always available with a listening ear.

WOMEN WANT TO FEEL HEARD AND UNDERSTOOD WHEN FACING A PROBLEM. INSTEAD OF TRYING TO SOLVE IT OR CHALLENGING HER FEELINGS, MEN NEED TO COMMUNICATE WITH EMPATHY.

That being said, a man can certainly help. Simply agreeing with a woman's feelings and showing understanding instead of trying to solve her problem—or worse, trying to argue with her feelings by disagreeing with her perception—is a huge help. She may or may not be perceiving

---

21. Ibid.

everything correctly, but listening intently and empathizing with how she feels will help her work through the situation when she feels less volatile or violated.

Women want to feel heard and understood when facing a problem. Instead of trying to solve it or challenging her feelings, men need to communicate with empathy. The problem will often dissipate.

WARNING: THIS IS NO TIME FOR LOGIC, SPOCK!

Are you a married man whose wife is pregnant, experiencing PMS, or going through menopause? Please understand that her hormones are fluctuating *and* her emotions may be heightened. When she comes to you with a problem, consider saying:

> "I'm so sorry that happened to you. You must have felt _____. I want to understand how you feel. What can I do to make it better?" *(Fill in the blank depending on the situation.)*

Then simply be there. Hold her or let her cry, but don't go into attorney mode and start to argue the other person's point or justify their actions. I say "the other person" because it's almost always going to be a relational issue that upset her.

If you argue the other person's position, she won't feel comforted and her hurt will be multiplied and projected toward you.

> *Rejoice with those who rejoice; mourn with those who mourn. Live in harmony with one another.* (Romans 12:15–16)

That Scripture gives good advice. Remind yourself that her incredible emotional makeup is her strength, but right now, it's got the best of her. She will work through it and your comfort will help her do that.

STRESS AND TESTOSTERONE

Too much stress can also create high levels of cortisol in men. Annis and Nesbitt say, "Elevated cortisol levels can have a draining effect on men as well, depleting their testosterone levels and increasing their blood pressure, anxiety, irritability, and fatigue. It can also cause weight gain in men."[22]

A man is more likely to become aggressive and angry *or* depressed and withdrawn with increased cortisol levels.

If you see these symptoms in someone you love, perhaps that man needs a getaway—a break from work or whatever's worrying him. That probably translates into solitude for him and not being forced to talk about it until he initiates the discussion. Send him out to fish at a creek, encourage him to watch a game on TV or sleep in the recliner—whatever you know he does to escape and needs to do to regain his strength, replenish his testosterone, and feel comforted. He will talk to you when he gets to that place and feels up to it.

Most men combat stress by resting and then talking; most women like to talk and then rest.

MOST MEN COMBAT STRESS BY RESTING AND THEN TALKING;
MOST WOMEN LIKE TO TALK AND THEN REST.

God designed men and women to be uniquely different as a gift to discover in each other, a complementary composition. If we choose to accept, attempt to understand, and honor the differences and appreciate the design, we can lighten each other's burdens, laugh together, solve problems, create life, and share in the gift of companionship and love.

22. Ibid.

5

VANITY, LOVE, AND THE NEW "S" WORD

We can't talk about men and women getting along without talking about what is almost always at the core of why they don't—*selfishness*. I always say, "Relationships aren't hard; selfishness is." In fact, do you know what causes most marriages to fail? Gary and I have sat down with thousands of couples through the years, and I can almost guarantee it's not what you think.

Most marriages fail because the *two* never become *one*. They move in together physically, but they still live totally separate lives. It's all about girls' night, guys' night, *my* money, *his* money… *my* time, *my* needs, *my* stuff.…

Gary and I have been shocked by the number of couples we have financially counseled who live totally separate financial lives. If you live like you and your spouse are living two separate lives, guess what? Eventually, you will! When we come together in marriage, we are one. It's no longer *mine* and *his*—it's *ours*. It's not always easy, but the effort of becoming *one* is so much better than the heartbreak of living as *two*.

Okay, okay, I'm going to get off of my soapbox… for now.

THE AGE OF SELFIES

The fact is, we live in the *I* time where feelings and selfies rule. I have many of them myself. Of my 91,000 pictures, I admit 9,100 are selfies. Yes, that's 10 percent.

I was raised in a time when no one would consider taking a picture of themselves. We struggled to ask another person to shoot our picture as it would be considered clearly vain. Parents or friends could take pictures on special occasions or family portraits, but that was Easter or Christmas, on vacation, or a birthday, just a few times a year. Camera film and development were considered expensive. As a child, I once shot an entire roll of film taking pictures of my kittens—and I was warned never to do it again.

I'm not sure if expense was the restraining force or a sense of modesty and self-control. Probably both. But just like everything else, advancing technology changed everything. With the smartphone and cloud storage, unlimited pictures could be shot and accessible without restraint—for free! (Or so the marketers want us to think. But clearly, $800 phones, monthly fees, and cloud storage all add up.)

How did I make the transition from less than a hundred photos during my entire childhood and teens to 9,100 selfies? (I think I should start deleting right now!) Funny enough, I noticed each selfie has five or more of the same picture when I'm trying to get the *best* one. Don't judge me. I'll bet you do it too.

The way I have managed to adapt to selfies illustrates how the culture slowly breaks down norms and reforms our opinions about everything utilizing media, peer pressure, and our own tendency toward self-centeredness. When we come into any relationship with a "What's in it for me?" mindset, it's doomed to fail.

Relationships take work, and that work will never be perfectly divided between two people, whether in the workplace or in marriage. There are times when Gary is carrying more weight around the house, and there are times when I am. It's not about keeping score. We are on the same team, and we are working together to get the job done. When we come into relationships thinking "How can I bless them?" instead of a "How can I get something from them?" mindset, the game changes.

WHEN WE COME INTO RELATIONSHIPS THINKING "HOW CAN I BLESS THEM?" INSTEAD OF A "HOW CAN I GET SOMETHING FROM THEM?" MINDSET, THE GAME CHANGES.

THE NEW "S" WORD

Popular magazines tell us what we should think about everything from sex to politics. With names like *Vanity Fair*, *Cosmopolitan*, *Self*, and *Allure*, it's obvious what the root of these popular brands comes down to: *me*. Their headlines, which are even more provocative, relate how we can lay a trap both sexually and politically to gain control and make people love us.

Number one in the country, *Cosmopolitan's* self-described positioning is, "Your source for the latest sex tips, celebrity news, dating and relationship help, beauty tutorials, fashion trends, and more." I was dismayed to discover that over half of the articles I perused had extreme political agendas mixed in. I'm not sure what those agendas have to do with beauty or fashion.

You will never change what you tolerate. —Joel Osteen

We may initially resist the culture's influence, but eventually, just like the selfie, we give in and change. Does giving in stop the pressure? No. Giving in doesn't satisfy the voices of vanity, self-centered pursuits, agendas, and wrongdoing. Lust or evil are never satisfied. For every step we back up and allow vain messages to encroach on us and advance forward, they keep pressing us to step back again… and again. That is the picture of compromise we all struggle to live in and against.

So, is there anything really wrong with vanity? What are its results?

*For where you have envy and selfish ambition, there you find disorder and **every evil practice**.* (James 3:16)

Submission is the new "S" word in today's culture. A brand consultant a few years back told me she had never seen a marriage like Gary's and mine. She wanted me to really focus in on telling people how to have healthy marriages, but said I should never talk about submission.

Huh?

That was just the first of a laundry list of things she told me I couldn't talk about. After that, I knew our working relationship had to end. She wanted the fruit I have in my life, but she didn't want me to talk about any of the *real* principles that gave me those results.

Well, friend, anyone who refuses to tell you about the beautiful power of *submission* isn't doing you any favors. When we refuse to submit to the authorities in our lives, we rebel against God's authority as well, and the Bible says we open the door to disorder and every evil practice. Ambition without submission creates chaos and confusion.

AMBITION WITHOUT SUBMISSION CREATES CHAOS AND CONFUSION.

Now, I am not talking about abusive submission inflicted by legalism. When people talk about submission, it often seems like they are on one side of the ditch or the other—they are advocating rebellion, or they are advocating this type of religious submission that says you can't do anything and completely silences the call of God on your life.

Did you know that submission means to "come under the loving care of" someone else? It's easy to submit to the authorities in our lives when we understand this.

Jesus, who was perfect, consistently showed us how He submitted Himself to the Father. He said, *"For I did not speak on my own, but the Father who sent me commanded me to say all that I have spoken"* (John 12:49).

I have always been a very motivated, determined personality. That's not a bad thing. That's how God made me, and it has helped Gary and me accomplish a lot of the things we have done. If you are a driven woman, there is nothing wrong with that. God gave you that gift of ambition; it's only bad when it isn't submitted under the loving care of the authorities in your life.

And yes, if you are married, that means submitting to your husband's loving wisdom. That may not be the popular opinion, but I didn't say it, God did. Ephesians 5:22 says, *"Wives, submit yourselves to your own husbands as you do to the Lord."*

God also gave husbands this command: *"In this same way, husbands ought to love their wives as their own bodies. He who loves his wife loves himself"* (Ephesians 5:28). How hard is it to submit to someone who loves you and is watching out for you just as much as he would for himself?

If you look at both of these pieces together, you see the beautiful picture God designed for marriage. It's supposed to be a selfless union of two people putting the other first, a small glimpse of God's love for us. Instead of focusing on what *we* get out of the relationship, God is calling us to look at what we can give in the relationship.

> *In everything I did, I showed you that by this kind of hard work we must help the weak, remembering the words the Lord Jesus himself said: "It is more blessed to give than to receive."* (Acts 20:35)

THE TRUTH ISN'T ALWAYS POPULAR

Kanye West admitted he had written the dirtiest song he could conjure intentionally to make money. He played the game and scored a financial win.

> *The devil took [Jesus] to a very high mountain and showed him all the kingdoms of the world and their splendor. "All this I will give you," he said, "if you will bow down and worship me."* (Matthew 4:8–9)

After ill-gotten gain and success almost destroyed him, West decided to take a different turn in his life and music. He was accepted by the world until he no longer would rap their tune; as he started to make gospel music, a vicious attack was unleashed. It came from the political left and religious people with a form of godliness without power.

Jesus said, *"If the world hates you, keep in mind that it hated me first"* (John 15:18).

There was far less criticism for the previously highly sexualized content that Kanye West rapped, but gospel music? Now that's dangerous and highly alarming to those with an agenda that involves something akin to biblical Sodom and Gomorrah or Noah's contemporaries before the flood. These evil forces of rebellion against God have been at work ever since Satan hissed in the garden, *"Did God really say...?"*

WHEN SUBMISSION IS WRONG

Scripture calls Satan *"the god of this world"* (2 Corinthians 4:4 ESV). This world loves to worship at his throne... but not without consequences. The ultimate price for sin is death, now and eternally. Satan knows this, but most people ignore it in their desire for acceptance and inclusion.

THE ULTIMATE PRICE FOR SIN IS DEATH,
BUT MOST PEOPLE IGNORE THIS IN THEIR DESIRE
FOR ACCEPTANCE AND INCLUSION.

The attempt to break us down and change social norms has never moved with greater intensity than in Hitler's Nazi Germany.

Yad Vashem, the World Holocaust Remembrance Center in Jerusalem, contains hundreds of videos, pictures, and artifacts that share the stories of adults, children, business owners, families, and clergy whose lives were taken from them, destroyed without cause because of their faith. It's hard for us to understand how Hitler's agenda could change the hearts of people to agree and carry out such vile behaviors as were perpetrated in the concentration camps, such as starvation and gas chambers, but it did. The shocking part was how he manipulated Christians to agree with his barbarism by blaming the Jews for the crucifixion and every other evil of society. It was propaganda at its worst! Never mind that Jesus and His early followers were all Jewish and that the foundations of Christianity are rooted in Jesus's following the teachings of Judaism. Anti-Semitic rhetoric, cartoons, and propaganda blamed every social ill on the Jewish people. They became the scapegoat and Hitler justified destroying or seizing their property and taking seven million lives.

Thirty years after Hitler's death, Pol Pot came to power in Cambodia. I have ministered to the beautiful people of this Asian nation on a couple of occasions. Pol Pot, who ruled from 1975 to 1979, caused the deaths of an estimated 1.5 to 2 million Cambodians due to starvation, execution, disease, or overwork. An entire generation was wiped out and millions of orphaned children were left to fend for themselves. Cambodia is recovering from such evil and many millennial Cambodian men and women are following Christ and learning biblical family models and patterns they missed as children.

The world has endured many atrocities since Satan tempted Adam and Eve. All of them come from failure to submit to God. Rather than embracing His plans and His love, people have listened to the *father of lies*. Satan declared:

> *I will ascend to the heavens; I will raise my throne above the stars of God; I will sit enthroned on the mount of assembly.… I will ascend above the tops of the clouds; I will make myself like the Most High.*
> (Isaiah 14:13–14)

Notice the devil kept saying, *"I will."* Powerful words. Pride and vanity emanate from this creature, Lucifer, who turned his role of leadership under God's authority into a place of treason. He led the angels under him into rebellion. As a result, a third of the angels were kicked out of heaven and exiled into the earth as fallen creatures of evil. (See Revelation 12.)

Eventually, God created man and woman and gave them dominion and authority over Satan and this sphere of recreated earth. They were to rule on behalf of His kingdom.

The man and woman were naked and not ashamed in this beautiful place of being known and fully known by one another and God. This was the three-cord strand of relationship that God created them to enjoy, to draw life from His love and give it to one another. They were complete.

It is a wonderful plan that I was reminded of while walking through the Sistine Chapel on a fall weekday, when crowds were few. In the relative solitude, I studied the magnificent ceiling frescoes by Michelangelo. Beside the famous image of God and Adam touching index fingers, Eve is depicted as coming forth out of a sleeping Adam and looking humbly upon her gracious Maker. It's easy to get the sense of God's heart to surprise Adam with this beautiful, delightful creation. Adam looks like a young man taking a nap who's about to discover the most wondrous gift a parent could give to surprise a child.

Eve was created to be Adam's truly equal companion, made in God's image, just as he was.

> The LORD God made a woman from the rib he had taken out of the man, and he brought her to the man. The man said, "This is now bone of my bones and flesh of my flesh; she shall be called 'woman,' for she was taken out of man." (Genesis 2:22–23)

Adam and Eve tended the garden together and God visited them in the cool of the evening, the best time of day. They experienced love, acceptance, peace, and provision until one day, the perpetrator of heaven's rebellion appeared in disguise and plotted to deceive Eve. Michelangelo painted a python-like creature wrapped around the forbidden tree from the ground up, with human-like face, chest, and hands reaching out to Eve. She knew this wasn't God or Adam and had no clue who this could be.

SATAN OFFERED EVE SOMETHING SHE ALREADY POSSESSED FROM GOD— LOVE, IDENTITY, WORTH, AND PROVISION—IN AN EFFORT TO STEAL IT.

The lying creature offered her something *she already possessed* in an effort to *steal* what she already had from God: love, identity, worth, and provision. It lied about God's goodness and character, questioning God's motives. *"Did God really say…?"* It tempted her to believe she was missing something, that God was withholding something great and marvelous. This deceiver tried to misconstrue God's Word and intentions as selfish. The enemy always accuses after his own heart.

I can almost hear one woman telling another, "He had the *nerve* to say that to you? You don't have to put up with that! You have your rights!" Talk-show hosts, books, magazines, music—so many of them find fault with marriage, men, monogamy, fidelity, motherhood, and trust. Ultimately, they ask, "Did God really say…?" Or worse, they say, "There is no God," or "We are all co-creators of the universe." The deceiver masquerades as an angel of light to destroy lives, just as he did with the first couple.

My people—infants are their oppressors, and women rule over them.
O my people, your guides mislead you and they have swallowed up the
course of your paths. (Isaiah 3:12 ESV)

The broken children, who have grown up without much guidance or instruction from mothers or fathers, look to lying leadership coiled up to strike. They are open to the deceptions of the enemy and seek answers from deceivers. They are looking for the love and value that were missing from home.

These generations of children have grown up raised by social media, violent video games, lyrics filled with filth, and godless liberal educational institutions that taught perversity and convinced them that socialism should be their battle cry. They have rejected their mothers and fathers as role models or voices in their lives. Hardened hearts consumed with anger, depression, violence, and grief fill these children whose innocence and childhood were stolen away.

The LORD was witness between you and the wife of your youth…your
companion and your wife by covenant. Did he not make them one,
with a portion of the Spirit in their union? And what was the one God
seeking? Godly offspring. (Malachi 2:14–15 ESV)

Without oneness in the home and parents representing God to the child, the deception comes full circle.

THE SEARCH FOR LOVE

We want to be loved and valued. That's the need of every person. We want others to recognize our value, too. But at what point is our craving for acceptance a crossover into vanity, taking the course of our lives out of God's garden of love and into our own wasteland of lack? Pain, hardship, poverty, and brokenness abound everywhere that rebellion and disobedience are heralded as truth. Simply look at the cities of our nation and those throughout history.

God is still looking at the hearts of men and women instead of religious presentations, popularity, or superficial accomplishments and facades. *"People look at the outward appearance, but the* LORD *looks at the heart"* (1 Samuel 16:7).

It's easy to believe appearances and voices, to get our answers from marketing, media, and the celebrity culture. But keep in mind, the driving force of their campaigns is to get your money and make you a pauper so they end up owning you. They are masters at manipulating human nature. They create divisions that magnify differences and offenses to manipulate men and women for their agendas and self-centered profits.

The wealthiest king of ancient times, Solomon experienced it all—and had it all. Yet in his writings, he points out the vanity of selfishness:

> *When I surveyed all that my hands had done and what I had toiled to achieve, everything was meaningless, a chasing after the wind; nothing was gained under the sun.... Without [God], who can eat or find enjoyment? To the person who pleases him, God gives wisdom, knowledge and happiness, but to the sinner he gives the task of gathering and storing up wealth to hand it over to the one who pleases God.*
> (Ecclesiastes 2:11, 25–26)

We can pursue the best of the world's promises, but in the end, what really matters? As women, we are sold so many products that are supposed to stop the aging process, cover our real or imagined defects, and offer us the fountain of youth. Fashion changes so fast that it is impossible to keep up with the current trends, which are all designed to create discontent within us. Our closets are full of what was yesterday, but give no hope for a tomorrow.

> *Charm is deceptive, and beauty is fleeting; but a woman who fears the* LORD *is to be praised.* (Proverbs 31:30)

No matter how hard you run after things, in the end, you cannot take it with you! The days on this earth are short and with all of our pursuit of beauty, fame, and wealth, women are still no happier. You can dress women up on the outside, but the statistics tell us a different story than the glamorous glossy magazine pictures sell us. Abortion, for example, is sold to us as being progressive and offering us freedom. Children murdered before or just after their birth is justified as a woman's right to her own body.

Yet statistics of post-abortion women dealing with increased mental health issues, suicidal tendencies, and depression demonstrate that this abhorrent "choice" goes directly against a woman's very nature of protection and concern for the welfare of her young.

A FRESH START

In a world where people's image of love is a form of immature self-gratification, it's no wonder that marriage and children are discarded, and breakups are viewed as more normal than lasting marriages, for these require giving instead of taking. God's plan for love sees a bigger picture in relationships and gives meaning to them. Without God's love, relationships at best will be based on the demand, "Give me what I want," and are sure to fail.

I really *love* house slippers and an occasional chocolate, but not the same way I love my husband. After a day of wearing heels, slippers are comfortable and give me a sense of relaxation. So does savoring a chocolate or a croissant. But *loving* these things is not the same as loving Gary. We use the word *love* so flippantly that we have lost its real meaning. I have worn out many pairs of house slippers and forgotten thousands of savored chocolates, but my marriage is never worn out or forgotten. I am committed to Gary in a covenant marriage. We must protect and invest in it, just as we protect and invest in God's love for us.

One of my greatest fears after my sinful choice of abortion as a teen was that I would not be able to have children. I felt as though I didn't deserve the opportunity to become a mother. So many women desire children who have not been able to conceive and a prior abortion is often the cause. Abortion is senseless and selfish, sold as our *right* as a woman. I exercised that "right" and it left me with nightmares and torment, fear and anguish. Fortunately, God's love and forgiveness helped me work through this trauma, as did Gary after we met and married.

WHEN WE COME TO CHRIST AND TURN TO HIM WITH ALL OUR HEARTS,
HE REMOVES THE PAST AND ANY BROKENNESS.

When we come to Christ and turn to Him with all our hearts, He removes the past and any brokenness. My own experience—and that of so many women I have had the blessing of knowing—is that the enemy attacks the area of our greatest restoration and joy.

I played with dolls as a young girl until a female teacher told me that such a pastime was beneath me as a woman. She held up a picture of vanity to me and offered me the forbidden, promoting it as an exciting adventure if I became a rebel like her. She made it look like something God or men withheld from me. *How dare they?* After my first hurtful relationship, I lost all sense of trust and embraced the confusion, rejecting God's words about my womanhood.

The Bible says, *"Women will be saved through childbearing"* (1 Timothy 2:15). It is clear that salvation comes only through Jesus Christ, as we surrender our vanity. However, I do believe that having children saved me from the lies and vanity of the earth-cursed system of selfishness. Children placed a demand on me like no other and gave me the greatest joy ever. Sharing this with my husband painted a deep picture of God's love and opened all the allegories of Scripture I would ever need to see, a parallel of God's love, forgiveness, sacrifice, and longing to see His children whole and happy in relationship with Him. Five children kept me busy, happy, and thankful that I could still be a wife and mother. The business pursuits, earnings, ministry, travel, speaking, and writing were all icing on the cake. You really can have your cake and eat it too if you follow God.

The root issue of women hating men or men debasing women is not simply a rejection of the opposite sex, but a rejection of God and His design. It is the desire to be independent of each other and, really, independent of God Himself. You will never find a God-adoring woman who is an angry feminist, or a righteous man who detests women… at least for very long. You simply can't be both because self-sufficiency and loathing for half the human race is the antithesis of submitting our lives to a sovereign Creator. In the feminist manifesto, men and God are lumped into the same category and neither are to be trusted. It's an assault on faith as much as it is a denouncement of males.

When I rejected the idea of men in my life, I resisted the idea of God directing my life as well. And when I came back to God, I opened my heart to a good man in my life and became his wife.

Trust in the LORD with all your heart and lean not on your own understanding; in all your ways submit to him, and he will make your paths straight. (Proverbs 3:5–6)

SELF-SUFFICIENCY IS A TRAP

God cannot direct people who lean on themselves instead of on Him. Fortunately, when I came to the end of me, God was there. I got to the end because each achievement left me emptier. After every performance, I was left with that sinking feeling that to be worthy of love, I would need to accomplish more, and repeat the performance again… and again… and again. I exhausted my resources and in brokenness, I cried out for help.

If we want to understand and fully lay hold of God's life for us, we must navigate relationships without a calloused heart.

They are darkened in their understanding and separated from the life of God because of the ignorance that is in them due to the hardening of their hearts. (Ephesians 4:18)

Ignorance comes from a hardened heart that either doesn't know or doesn't accept God's design for relationships and authority, His or any other. We must learn to shut out the other voices—sometimes even our own!

Love is not a feeling or accessed by vanity as we have been led to believe. It first must originate from God. God is love. He loves with a different kind of love than we do. Selfishness is not love. It isn't even self-love. It's a form of self-hatred. Selfishness creates loneliness and destroys love. It's the deceiver's attempt to make us think we can pursue our own way to find satisfaction.

SELFISHNESS IS THE DECEIVER'S ATTEMPT TO MAKE US THINK WE CAN PURSUE OUR OWN WAY TO FIND SATISFACTION.

Yes, I have about 9,000 more selfies than I should, but well over half of them are with Gary. I'm thankful to share life with him. I am the one who obviously enjoys photos, both taking them and reviewing them. I shoot them with one arm extended and thumb through them as I travel. They remind me of the wonderful blessings of love and family.

Although I originally rejected these gifts, they were given to me through His salvation. Together, Gary and I explore all the wonders God made in the earth and the wonder of the life that God has given to us and our family. I hold marriage as a holy plan between a man and woman who are learning to be holy, too.

6

MISCOMMUNICATION GETS US NOWHERE

Every superhero has incredible abilities and strengths, but they also have weaknesses. The goal is to maximize their strength and protect them from their weaknesses so they can beat the sinister forces of darkness. That's exactly how a power couple must operate, too.

Each person brings differing abilities into the marriage and working relationship. Communication is key to vision casting, setting goals, and strategizing how to reach them by determining *who will do what when.* Honestly, when Gary and I started in business thirty-eight years ago, we couldn't see all that we see today, but we saw pieces of it. And we didn't have a plan all written out for *how* or *who.* We both studied the business, attended meetings together, and started to jump into doing whatever was necessary to *win.*

Gary didn't say, "Drenda, it's your job to do this or that." We weren't that sophisticated. We knew where we wanted to go and both of us started doing what we saw would move the ball to the goalpost. But to be sure, there were some long discussions and dreaming sessions, whether on a road trip driving our kids to see Grandma at Christmastime or on a family vacation. At times, these discussions turned into the question, "What are we doing wrong?" But they always ended with course corrections and new hopes of how changes could take us that much closer to our goal.

I stepped into areas in our business that were natural strengths for me while Gary worked steadily in areas that were his. We weren't trying to prove anything or compete. We were trying to survive one more day to achieve our objective. If we didn't work, we didn't eat. He was completely commissioned and because I believed in him and I believed in our dreams, I did everything I could to learn, support, and work with him. It wasn't a drudgery. It was fun most of the time.

Vision is exciting and moving closer toward our dreams inspired us to deal with whatever personal struggles we had to tackle to make it. Dreams fuel your life and faith fuels your dreams. Our faith in God's Word and in each other made all the financial struggle surmountable. We were just one day closer to our common goals. I discovered my passions and gifts in serving our vision. We both became better because of the value we learned to place on each other.

Saying "I do" is not a guarantee there won't be conflict. You can expect there will be! That's just common sense. A magical pixie dust doesn't fall out of the sky to ensure you're never going to disagree, argue, or occasionally battle. Just don't let it become a war. War presumes the other person's motives and character are villainous and that they are about to strike. You live in a defensive posture if you believe this, waiting for the attack. No relationship, let alone a marriage, can survive in a war zone like this. You can live in pressure and battle outside in a war zone, but you can't believe that the person you live with is the enemy!

People who have lived through real wars have managed to keep their marriages intact, but they did so by pulling together and recognizing that the real enemy was not their spouse, but a much greater, more sinister force from outside. That's the protective shield we must fight with if we are to succeed. We must keep the darkness out and reject anything that tries to come against our love for our marriage partner.

Did Gary and I ever have conflict? Of course! And occasionally, we still do. But it's met with much more maturity and understanding today.

I would say the beginning of a vision and its fruition are the best part of the journey. There are some sticky situations in the middle that can be the hardest because you are working but aren't seeing the outcome you'd like. That's the pressure point when it's tempting to argue or blame the other person for the pressure. But we need to decide that we are not going to allow arguments to divide us. We can learn to disagree without demands or division.

Whether you're in a marriage or in a conference room, God is speaking to you through others. We share a dream and begin to speak words back and forth that create. God created everything that exists by speaking His Word and He placed that same creative force in each of us. Men and women succeeding together can give birth to a company, a product, or a child.

What words are we speaking and what dreams are created or destroyed by the power of our words? Words come from the heart and the heart gets pictures from what we meditate on. The messages we hear and pictures we see form our thoughts. Are we listening to the popular fads or timeless truths? Think and speak God's thoughts and promises to begin to change your communication.

ARGUMENTS, BATTLES, AND WAR

There's a difference between having an argument, a battle, or an all-out war. Disagreements can lead to arguments and this happens in every relationship at some point. Battles can originate from outside forces and come against the relationship or from within because of conflicting viewpoints. Hurts happen when we feel undervalued, misunderstood, not accepted, or unloved.

War is a different matter altogether. There was a war declared on men, women, and marriage by the enemy. The devil has used division and society's pro-this or anti-that movements that we have all been raised in and influenced by. If we come into any relationship with a preconceived lack of trust or already-formed conclusions, war breaks out when we really should be processing it as a disagreement. It's one of the reasons we have seen the divorce rate quadruple since the women's movement and why 75 percent of divorces are filed by women.

In times past, a couple was expected to have disagreements, kiss, and make up. Movies even depicted couples in heated arguments, the woman throwing plates in stubborn anger at an amused man. Later, of course, they kissed. People used to say half the fun of arguing was making up. That was in an era when divorce was not an option except in the most extreme cases. The fact that it wasn't *considered* an option made the couple reconcile their differences. If our preconceived idea is that men or women are bad and it's just a matter of time before they prove it, we keep looking for the evidence that we're right. Or if we believe that life is easier without the opposite sex because they make unreasonable demands on us, that will most certainly be the trait we magnify in them.

IF OUR PRECONCEIVED IDEA IS THAT SOMETHING IS TRUE, WE WILL KEEP LOOKING FOR THE EVIDENCE THAT WE'RE RIGHT.

Our ministry used to receive sample books from a Christian distributor. I couldn't read them all, so I'd share them with our volunteers. There was a woman who volunteered weekly to help our girls' ministry and put forth great effort to care for them. I decided to give her one of these sample books about the power of love. I included a note thanking her for caring and serving.

To my surprise, a week later, she came up to me after service. I thought she might acknowledge the gift or want to talk, feeling more connected. Boy, was I ever surprised! She was in attack mode.

"Do you think I don't know how to love people? Who do you think you are!?"

Ouch! I began to backpedal and apologized sincerely for the misunderstanding. I assured her that I didn't give her the book because I thought she had issues loving people, but rather because I could tell by her investment that she genuinely loved the girls in the ministry and valued investing into people's lives. She backed down and walked away.

It upset me that my desire to encourage and befriend her had been so misread. What I thought and expected were different than the way she received my friendly gesture.

A few weeks later, she came to me and said she overreacted, but she had heard unfavorable things about me and my husband. She had misread my gift based on the false information that another person had given to her. *Ouch again!* Her preconceived idea about me made her find supporting evidence that I was trying to hurt her instead of bless her and she drew the wrong conclusion.

Isn't that what happens so often in relationships, especially if we are filtering things through a past hurt or false information? Sincere, meaningful communication is the remedy, and how we communicate with each other is just as important.

There has to be time set aside to communicate well. For me and Gary, our long road trips proved to be a great way to break down barriers and be isolated long enough to get past communication hindrances. If you're in lockdown for fifty hours of driving, there *will* be communication. No board meeting or planning could have accomplished what these vision sessions on the road produced. We lost all sense of time, but all pressures and distractions were left behind.

We have learned to call this *going to the mountain*. Every couple needs time to hear God. We literally drove to the mountains most of the time, but it's more about getting away so we can listen for His voice. Jesus had to get away to a quiet place to hear His Father and so do we. The problem is often not that God isn't speaking, but that we can't hear Him with thought-cluttered heads and clamoring noises.

EVERY COUPLE HAS A MISSION. THEY JUST HAVEN'T ALWAYS TAKEN THE TIME TO GET IN TOUCH WITH EACH OTHER TO DISCOVER IT.

We have found that God uses people often to speak to us. He gives one person a piece of the puzzle, another person the interlocking piece, and when we talk we put them together, voila! A masterpiece comes forth. So many times, there's an aching void inside of each person holding the piece, with no one to talk to and express what they see. You can live with someone, but not have real heart exposure. We can lose sight of the other person's heart or feel alone if we don't *go to the mountain* at least annually to revisit our purpose as a couple, recognize the sinister forces that are at odds with our mission, and create a strategy to win against them for the sake of mankind.

Every couple has a mission. They just haven't always taken the time to get in touch with each other to discover it. What did you dream of doing? What has taken the place of your dream? How can you find it again? Conflict occurs more often because we lose sight of our dreams together. It's amazing how fast we can throw aside our differences when the vision speaks louder. Too many couples are bored with life and become bored with each other because they're not out saving the day together.

There are some keys that will help you communicate successfully. Recognize that if you jump to conclusions quickly, they most always will be flawed, or your response will be way off even if your conclusion is accurate. Slow down and hear the facts or feelings of the other person before you decide. Each sex and individual person has filters they hear through and ways they communicate.

COMMUNICATION STYLES

Men and women have very different communication styles. No surprise there! This can open the door for misunderstandings and strife when we don't learn to *walk in each other's shoes* or understand that people can't read our minds.

Women will often hint at something they want or need instead of directly saying exactly what's on their minds. Sometimes, they will ask a question to make a suggestion or dance around the subject without being direct. I know it's silly, but hey, it happens.

"Do you think we should go out to dinner on Friday?" is actually her way of saying, "I'd like to go, but I don't want to force it on you." Sometimes, this isn't clear to him. Men generally don't read between the lines like most women do with one another. They rarely pick up on the suggestion because they see it simply as a question. If he fails to understand that she really wants to go out, she may become offended or hurt at his insensitivity. But he wasn't trying to be inattentive.

No one should beat around the bush when communicating with another. Make your thoughts and feelings clear by saying what you mean. He knows exactly what she wants when she says, "I would very much like to go out to dinner on Friday. How about you?"

NO ONE SHOULD BEAT AROUND THE BUSH WHEN COMMUNICATING WITH ANOTHER. MAKE YOUR THOUGHTS AND FEELINGS CLEAR BY SAYING WHAT YOU MEAN.

Most men aren't super sleuths, but women often force them to look for clues in the conversation when they give vague hints. If a woman makes a tentative suggestion, the man should ask himself, *What is she really trying to say?* To guys, it's a little absurd, but the woman doesn't want to be demanding so she hints at her desire, thinking she has planted the seed. If she feels slighted, it will backfire on both of them.

If women are indirect, men are typically very direct. He will often appear blunt to her in his communication. He may say what he wants in as few words as possible and, to her, this can come across as rude. It's man's innate laser focus that causes his directness. He bluntly goes for the bottom line. If good manners are employed, neither is right or wrong; they're just different.

When Gary and I talk, he usually says the statements that make up the framework of our discussion and I often fill in the anatomy or strategy. I process my thoughts with words. He thinks and then speaks.

I observed two men in a conversation recently. There were very long pauses between their comments. Each would physically turn his head away from the other and stare off somewhere, thinking. Then he would turn back and speak again. I was fascinated. They reminded me so much of Rodin's famous sculpture of the Thinker each time they had to answer. Their long pauses made me want to jump up and answer for them. They were processing in their minds, not with their words.

Being direct can be a great strength for men, but they need to be careful not to sound demanding or unfeeling. Depending on the situation, a man's directness and a woman's empathetic communication style can be huge assets to your team. Remember, your differences are what make you succeed together!

BEING DIRECT CAN BE A GREAT STRENGTH FOR MEN, BUT THEY NEED TO BE CAREFUL NOT TO SOUND DEMANDING OR UNFEELING.

Gary may say, "I want to make the President's Club this year." I ask what the reward is, then I begin to ask many questions about what it requires. *How close are we? What can we change?*

The more I understand the issue or problem, the easier it is for me to come up with some ideas he couldn't see, being so close to it. Sometimes the process that has always been used isn't the one that we need now to perform at a higher level. I give him many things to think about. Gary doesn't like change, but I need it. So if change is on the agenda, God will use me to start rooting out what is going on. Gary helps us stay steady since too much change can create chaos. We have learned this ebb and flow, but it takes time to figure out your unique working relationship. So give it time.

I'm so glad Gary isn't changing every day. His ability to keep repeating the same actions methodically helps us chip away at the day-to-day work to get us one step closer to our dream. My creativity sees what is and figures a way to change it to make it what we want. I change décor, clothes, and style consistently, but Gary is happy to wear the same favorite shirts. It drives me bonkers to see the same old red shirt every day on vacation, but for him it's comfort. The upside is that he is always happy to come home to the same old wife. Ha!

Our perspectives could be different but our goal is almost always the same or very close. It's more important that we agree on the big rocks than the methods to get there. Money can motivate Gary more than me. Money's reward for me is how I can spend it to get something for our family, whether an experience or something to enjoy together. But we are both more motivated by the cause or mission than money. Helping families build a great life and learn how to live by God's principles is far more motivating for us than finances. We see our business and ministry as ways to carry out that passion.

Developing communication that is consistent and inviting stops misunderstandings and helps you both realize your passion and satisfaction. We are really managing personalities and differences for success. The effort is worth the reward.

LEARN TO LEAVE SOME WORDS OUT OF YOUR VOCABULARY. PHRASES LIKE,
"YOU ALWAYS..." OR "YOU NEVER..."
PUT THE OTHER PERSON IMMEDIATELY ON THE DEFENSIVE.

Learn to leave some words out of your vocabulary. Phrases like, "You always..." or "You never..." put the other person immediately on the defensive. Learning to listen more, talk less, and be slower to decide have become important areas for me to work on. Gary has had to learn to speak more often so that I am not playing twenty questions to find out what's going on. It's an effort on both of our parts to both listen and speak with words that affirm the other's needs both intimately and in business situations.

If our communication starts to get frustrating, we have had to step away for a minute, take a time-out, pray, and then discuss our differences of opinion. Good communication requires time, effort, understanding, and avoiding attitudes or phrases that create conflict or the other person to clam up and go silent. The goal is to create unity and ultimately good relationships and decision-making, not *winning* the conversation. Nothing positive comes from threats, control, belittling, or trying to put the other person in their place.

Years ago during an intense push in business, Gary and I were both tired, having worked many hours with few breaks. I was frustrated by his silence. Obviously, *he* was too tired to talk, but because *I* was tired, I felt the need to talk to unwind and reconnect with him after weeks of busyness. I got upset that he was disengaged from me. He kind of laughed in a way that I felt was sarcastic or mocking, which added insult to injury. I began to cry. Instead of taking the defense and justifying himself, Gary quickly realized my need to feel close to him because I was emotionally and physically tired. So he apologized.

Often, communication is more about reading someone's emotions rather than their words. Are they exhausted? Are they upset about something? Do they feel lonely because you have been busy recently?

One of the *most* important lessons Gary and I have learned after years of marriage is that when you or your spouse is tired, be extra careful in your communication and give extra grace to them. It's easy to fall into strife when you are tired, angry, lonely, or hungry. Save intense conversations for later and extend lots of grace!

IT'S EASY TO FALL INTO STRIFE WHEN YOU ARE TIRED, ANGRY, LONELY, OR HUNGRY. SAVE INTENSE CONVERSATIONS FOR LATER AND EXTEND LOTS OF GRACE!

We need to learn to handle disagreements before they become arguments and stop arguments before they break out into destructive battles or wars.

7

THE SECRET TO RESOLVING CONFLICT IN RELATIONSHIPS

When I think about women and men succeeding together, I also think about the spiritual warfare that comes against us in marriage. Gary and I had to learn to not let strife come between us. We started to recognize that our oneness had to be protected in order for us to be successful. We learned how to not let our focus be reduced to conflicts over minor issues when our destiny was so much more important.

Satan is after the power of agreement, especially among spouses. He works to pit you against each other, so you aren't in unity working together against him. The Bible reminds us:

> For our struggle is not against flesh and blood, but against the rulers, against the authorities, against the powers of this dark world and against the spiritual forces of evil in the heavenly realms.
>
> (Ephesians 6:12)

No matter what you're dealing with in your marriage today, don't forget that your spouse isn't the enemy. Stand on the Word of God and speak it into your situation.

So many couples talk about how hard marriage is, but marriage isn't the issue. Marriage only reveals what's *already* inside of us. The real issue is our desire to do things *our* way, when and how *we* want. Marriage is God's plan to help us see ourselves in the mirror of how we treat others. Without it, we tend to just become more self-centered and demanding, which ultimately shows up in every relationship. You can see this so clearly in our culture. We need strong marriages and homes again to save America and the world from self-destruction. Children need the security and love that strong marriages bring.

When I look back at the beginning of my marriage, I know *it* wasn't hard—*we* were.

I'm personally grateful that although we sometimes still disagree, Gary and I have worked on a strong, rewarding relationship that has kept us from becoming hard-hearted and stubborn. It's tenderized the rough in us and brought out the good. We are better people with a better life because of our marriage to one another and our commitment to God.

FIVE STRATEGIES TO RESOLVE CONFLICT

Here are five powerful strategies to resolve conflict in your marriage and walk in unity with your spouse. These can also be helpful in any other relationship.

1. PUT YOURSELF IN THEIR SHOES

I can do things you cannot, you can do things I cannot; together we can do great things.   —Mother Teresa

Gary loves to go deer hunting. At the beginning of our marriage, I resented that. At the time, we were living in an old, broken-down farmhouse and we had little kids running around. I thought, *Why is he leaving me here to go hunting when there are so many things to get done?*

Meanwhile, Gary had spent a week trying to provide for our family and was feeling the pressure of our finances weighing on him. Besides trying to provide food for us by getting a deer, he thought, *I need a break. Why does she always have things for me to do when I want to go hunting?*

This is a classic example of how the enemy divides us. He wants you to focus on your needs, your issues, and your problems. He wants to pit you against each other instead of being in unity and working together against him. As long as Satan can divide us, he can conquer our marriages, our families, our workplaces, our churches, and our society. Selfishness asks, *How will this affect* me? Love asks, *How will this affect* them?

SELFISHNESS ASKS, HOW WILL THIS AFFECT ME? LOVE ASKS, HOW WILL THIS AFFECT THEM?

Gary and I had to learn to understand each other. I knew hunting was important to him because God created men with the desire to provide for their families and I had to learn to accept that. Gary had to learn to recognize the times when I needed his support around the house. When we learned to understand where the other person was coming from, our communications improved. I stopped saying, "You always…" and "You never…" because those phrases stop communication. Those words are so judgmental, they can come out like curses.

I also had to learn to be honest when I was upset about something rather than to let it bottle up inside. There's an expression that women are like volcanoes—they have to let off small eruptions or they explode.

2. KNOW WHEN TO LET THINGS GO

Be selective in your battles; sometimes peace is better than being right.
—Ritu Ghatourey

I asked one of my mentors—whose life and ministry are more accomplished than most—how she and her husband, both strong leaders, have managed together. She said, "Know when to back down. Pick your moment. Men are singular in focus so if you try and talk to them when they're focused on something else, it's useless. He's in his box!"

Her husband gave a similar answer. With a cheeky smile on his face, he said, "Back down sooner than later."

Satan is after the power of agreement because strife opens the door to him. When Gary and I were tempted to argue in the early years of our marriage, we would look at each other and say, "I'd rather prosper." It was immature, but it was our cue to let things go instead of arguing.

Sometimes, our greatest strength in dealing with conflict is knowing when to back down, walk it off, or take a breather. Ask yourself, "Is this really something worth fighting over? Will I care about this situation a year from now?"

WHEN STRIFE TRIES TO ENTER THE SCENE,
KNOW WHEN YOU NEED TO WALK IT OFF OR TAKE A BREATHER
BEFORE YOU SAY SOMETHING YOU CAN'T TAKE BACK.

When strife tries to enter the scene, know when you need to walk it off or take a breather before you say something you can't take back. We have to remember we aren't trying to *win* the conversation; we are simply trying to come to an agreement. That often means we must learn to meet in the middle.

3. DIVORCE OR WALKING AWAY ISN'T AN OPTION

Make it your goal to create a marriage that feels like the safest place on earth.   —Greg Smalley

Divorce, walking away from a friendship, or refusing to be on a project with a coworker should never be an option. Gary and I have never talked about divorce or even thought about it. For us, it's not a possibility. When you use divorce as a power play in heated conversations with your spouse, you compromise the foundation of your relationship.

When someone asked Dream City Church pastor Tommy Barnett how he has stayed married for more than fifty-five years, he said, "I'd rather fight than switch!" Ha!

Jesus replied, "Moses permitted you to divorce your wives because your hearts were hard. But it was not this way from the beginning."
(Matthew 19:8)

People's hearts become hard when hurts turn into anger and then bitterness.

*Make every effort to live in peace with everyone and to be holy; without holiness no one will see the Lord. See to it that no one falls short of the grace of God and that **no bitter root grows up to cause trouble and defile many**.* (Hebrews 12:14–15)

We can stop many divorces simply by getting to the root of the issue: bitterness, stubbornness, and an unforgiving spirit.

WHEN YOU USE DIVORCE AS A POWER PLAY IN HEATED CONVERSATIONS WITH YOUR SPOUSE, YOU COMPROMISE THE FOUNDATION OF YOUR RELATIONSHIP.

A healthy marriage should be a safe place where we can talk through issues without worrying about the other person threatening to walk out the door. Bringing up the idea of divorce in arguments will make both you and your spouse feel insecure and unsafe in your relationship. It often puts a hurdle between spouses that is difficult to remove even after the heat of the moment is gone.

4. MAKING A CASE

Because Gary and I are spiritually and philosophically aligned, our disagreements are not caused by a difference in beliefs. Instead, they're about life's decisions or distinctive perspectives. I've learned through the years to make my case when I feel strongly about a direction or issue. If it's not a big deal, I don't make it one. There have been times when I felt I knew a direction was from God or had a strong desire that I learned to make my case to help Gary see my viewpoint. Likewise he has had to do the same. We have smaller areas that are unnecessary to consult each other, but if it's anything large, directional, or costly, we do not decide without the other's consent.

Respect is paramount to make your case. *Nasty gets us nowhere!* I may have pulled those attitudes out in our earlier days, but I quickly learned that I didn't win even though I may have gotten my way. Because I learned to approach our differences with respect, he started to hear me and respect my heart.

> *An excellent wife… is far more precious than jewels. The heart of her husband trusts in her.* (Proverbs 31:10–11)

I appeal to Gary's sense of logic. Why do I think this direction will benefit him, our marriage, our family, or finances? I appeal to his sense of desire to profit. What will it cost compared to the benefit it will bring? I give him all of the information and research he needs to make an informed decision. If it's not an issue that falls into a benefit versus cost decision, but rather a desire I have, I speak to his desire to make me happy, or my desire to make *him* happy. Then we discuss my feelings or needs. I don't manipulate to get what I want; I simply state my case. There's give and take in every relationship. We come to an agreement and if the timing isn't now, we make an alternative plan.

5. PRAY TOGETHER AND FOR EACH OTHER

Rather than set aside daily time for prayer, I pray constantly and spontaneously about everything I encounter on a daily basis.
—Thomas Kinkade

Prayer only takes a few seconds, but it has the power to change the very course of our future. It's our superpower in faith, but one of the easiest things to put on the back burner in our day.

The moments when we should pray the most are often the times when we pray the least, such as when we're struggling to communicate with our spouse. In those moments when we're angry, upset, and tired of trying to talk to each other, often the last thing we think about is praying for the other person. We don't want to talk to them, let alone pray for them.

Prayer has the power to change atmospheres, hearts, and minds. When we're having a conflict with our spouse, that's when we need prayer the most. I love what Stormie Omartian wrote in her book *The Power of a Praying Wife*:

I Don't Even Like Him—How Can I Pray for Him? Have you ever been so mad at your husband that the last thing you wanted to do was pray for him? So have I. It's hard to pray for someone when you're angry or he's hurt you. But that's exactly what God wants us to do. If He asks us to pray for our *enemies*, how much more should we be praying for the person with whom we have become one and are supposed to love? But how do we get past the unforgiveness and critical attitude? The first thing to do is be completely honest with God. In order to break down the walls in our hearts and smash the barriers that stop communication, we have to be totally up-front with the Lord about our feelings. We don't have to "pretty it up" for Him. He already knows the truth. He just wants to see if we're willing to admit it and confess it as disobedience to His ways. If so, He then has a heart with which He can work.[23]

As a husband and wife, you have to come to the place of unity. It may take some time and some work, but it's worth it. Changes in your family are going to start from the head down—from you and your husband, from your marriage, and then to your children and family. Praying *for* your spouse is one of the most important habits you can cultivate in your day. Praying *with* your spouse is one of the most important habits you can cultivate in your life.

PRAYING WITH YOUR SPOUSE IS ONE OF THE MOST IMPORTANT HABITS YOU CAN CULTIVATE IN YOUR LIFE.

So let me ask you: how is your prayer life right now? Are you praying for your spouse daily? Are you praying *with* your spouse daily?

I encourage you to release God's power and love into your marriage. Trust God and turn your situation over to Him. Please meditate on the words of this prayer. Pray out loud and personally commit to uphold unity in your marriage:

Father, I thank You for my marriage and for my spouse. I thank You for unity even in hard times, and I pray that You bless our

23. Stormie Omartian, *The Power of a Praying Wife* (Eugene, OR: Harvest House Publishers, 2014).

marriage. I come into agreement with my spouse, and I release Your power into our situation. I thank You that we learn to love like You do and we communicate with understanding, in Jesus's name. Amen!

8

SAY THIS, NOT THAT—A CHEAT SHEET

Love covers, protects, and believes the best. In order to share Christ's love with each other, there are some things all of us should *avoid* saying or doing, and other things that we *should* do or say. Before we get into specifics that are helpful for women and men when communicating with their spouses, here are some general do's and don'ts for everyone.

WE ALL SHOULD AVOID

- Attacking, complaining, or criticizing in any form. This is never a constructive way to bring change.

- Bringing up past mistakes or making the other person feel incompetent.

- Criticizing someone's family or the way in which they were raised. They may bring these issues up for discussion, but respect their right to talk about it without joining in. Our parents, siblings, and other relatives are always a part of us, no matter what their shortcomings.

- Reminding the other person, "You were wrong the last time." Such a statement often makes a man lose his confidence, while it tends to make a woman angry.

- Bringing up a past sin so that the person feels they must repent or do penance. Guilt and shame are destroyers in any relationship.

- Making fun of their ideas, dreams, or goals.

+ Embarrassing someone with stories of their mistakes, failures, or personal problems.

ALL SPOUSES SHOULD AVOID

+ Belittling your spouse in front of the children or telling the kids about your spouse's faults.

+ Letting others know how unhappy you are with your spouse through snide little comments or sarcastic jokes.

+ Telling your spouse who you could have married instead or comparing them to other people.

+ Disregarding their requests or feelings about something and doing it anyway.

+ Huffing, puffing, snorting, slamming doors, throwing things, hiding in the bathroom or workshop, driving away, pitching temper tantrums, yelling, name-calling, scolding, and threatening to leave or divorce your spouse.

+ Using Scripture like a sword to kick their legs out from under them.

+ Overspending to get even or out of disrespect.

+ Thinking disrespectful thoughts about your spouse.

+ Demeaning their sexual performance, desire, or lack of desire.

+ Ignoring your spouse's opinion and being stubborn when discussing issues.

WE ALL SHOULD

+ Learn to say, "I'm sorry." Pride is ugly and will destroy any relationship. Accept that you make mistakes too.

+ Use manners when you speak to the other person.

+ Let them know how much they are appreciated.

+ Release their faults and give them to God. If they really are faults, God knows the best way to handle them.

+ Give the other person seventy times seven opportunities when they need forgiveness. One day, you'll need it, too, so be forgiving.

SPOUSES SHOULD

+ Praise your spouse and their efforts often. When you're with other people, build up your spouse's efforts and share the appreciation you feel.

+ Honor your spouse with your eyes, thoughts, and words. Don't make them feel like they have to compete with other people.

+ Respect your spouse and uphold their authority to your children. It's important that your children respect both of their parents.

+ Make eye contact when your spouse talks. You know—those adoring eyes you used to look at them with before you were married.

+ Tell them when you have a need and what they can do to meet it.

+ Pray for each other daily.

+ Be their best friend and put them first before others, including parents and children.

+ Take time to listen to each other.

+ Do tasks that alleviate stress for each other.

+ Share interests and hobbies.

+ Tell your spouse how blessed you are to be married to them.

+ Leave notes of encouragement praising them.

+ Show complete acceptance of them just like they are.

+ Assume the best if they fail to meet your expectations.

+ Examine your own heart ten times as much as you examine theirs.

COMMUNICATION TIPS FOR WIVES

Since women are often more verbal than their spouses, it's easy to manipulate or dominate their husbands by outtalking them. A wife has the power to make her husband feel like a *winner* or a *loser* simply with her words. She can make him feel like he can never say or do the right thing, or she can make him feel like he can conquer the world. Her words have the power to speak life and death to her husband's heart.

A wife can free her husband to be himself if she learns to speak his language.

A man needs to be admired and praised for his contribution to the marriage, his family, and his work. He needs to feel honored and respected, particularly by his wife and family. Don't deprive him of that and tempt him to look elsewhere for the appreciation he needs. You may think, *Oh, my husband's just ol' Joe, nobody special.* But chances are, there's someone out there who would love to have ol' Joe by her side. You should be that woman!

WIVES IN PARTICULAR SHOULD AVOID

+ Refusing to be his partner by making him go it alone in life.

+ Saying, "I told you so… if you'd just listened to me," or always having a better idea than his way. Remember, there's more than one way to do any job.

+ Reminding him of how he failed last time so you should be able to control the decisions.

+ Rolling your eyes, making demeaning gestures, sighs, or comments.

+ Giving him the silent treatment to punish him and ultimately control him.

+ Using sex as a reward or punishment for his behavior.

+ Taking control over the finances because he messed up before.

+ Mothering him, scolding him, and critiquing his every move.

+ Complaining or whining about how much he works or doesn't do enough to help out.

+ Reminding him of how much you have to do without because of his lack of provision.

+ Pressuring him financially, which stifles him with fear of failure.

+ Finishing his sentences, doing all the talking, or pressuring him to talk or answer you immediately.

THE ULTIMATE TEST

Ask yourself, "Would I treat Jesus Christ this way?" If it isn't appropriate for the Lord, it isn't appropriate for your husband.

TIPS ESPECIALLY FOR WIVES

+ See him off with warm, loving encouragement, and welcome him back the same way.

+ Invest in him and his dreams.

+ Admire him—his physique, his strength, his skills, his work, his personality, his character… any and every good quality.

+ Desire him sexually and let him know it.

+ If he has to work long hours for a season, support him. If you're in a position to work alongside him, do so.

+ Have fun together. Play and be active!

+ Be patient with him if he isn't talking. Your criticism will push him away.

+ Free him to succeed. A man cannot succeed at anything else if he's always having to jump through hoops for his wife.

+ Build his confidence. Men can't do anything without it.

+ Be sensitive when he needs to be alone or isn't ready to talk.

+ When you're discouraged, let him know it's not his fault and he doesn't have to fix anything; give him a listening ear and a hug.

+ Be patient with him; recognize that he will eventually value your contribution and praise you at the city gates. (See Proverbs 31.)

+ Be understanding of his pressures—physically, financially, emotionally, and sexually.

+ Make him a list if it's more than one item.

+ Get spiritual food for your household, so you set a tone of peace and faith.

+ Serve him food, drinks, and back rubs, whatever you can do to show him that you love and honor him. Remember, he needs your respect and admiration to feel confident.

COMMUNICATION TIPS FOR HUSBANDS

By design, God created a woman to be special, to *complement* her husband. She is to come under his protection and receive his care and love. As the husband does this, his wife responds with even more love.

A breakdown in communication styles and failure to understand her needs causes some women to stop seeing their husbands as a priority in their lives. A woman often begins to give this place of prominence to her children, her career, church activities, or another man. She can break off the relationship in her heart and yet remain married. Most husbands are shocked when their wives leave them. A man will often say he had no idea his wife was unhappy. He assumes she's happy because she pours herself into her family or a career; since his needs are so different from hers, he can be totally unaware and insensitive to her struggle. Ironically, the wife will say she tried over and over to communicate her needs and hurts.

As a man, you are called by God to *lay down your life for your wife* the way Christ did for the church. *Put her first.* Put aside your pride. Instead of seeing her as a competitor who you have to beat at the game of life, humble yourself and be willing to accept responsibility. Turn that responsibility over to the Lord in prayer, and ask Him for the answers.

THE ULTIMATE TEST

Ask yourself, "How would Jesus handle the same situation I'm in?" Men represent Jesus to their wives and families. They will give account to Him for the way they treat their wives. Ask yourself, "Is she my priority? Do I do what is best, even if it means saying no to something that would harm her?"

TIPS ESPECIALLY FOR HUSBANDS

+ Make time to communicate with your wife. Women need to talk just to express themselves. It doesn't mean you have to fix the situation for her. She just needs you to serve as a sounding board. Date nights, walks, and time alone together enable her to receive your undivided attention.

+ Look her in the eye and hold her hand when you talk to her. Let your eyes show how you love and admire her.

+ Reassure her when she is discouraged.

+ Listen when she talks just to talk. Conversation doesn't have to accomplish anything for it to be worthwhile to her. Women build relationships by talking. She needs to hear your feelings, pressures, or concerns, too. Try using word pictures or stories, something she can relate to. This often makes it easier for men and women to relate to each other.

+ Look for opportunities to say "I love you," and say it every day. Use birthdays, special events, surprise dates, surprise cards, and flowers to communicate this. Statistics show that a woman needs at least fifteen affirming touches, words, or signs of your love every day.

+ Give her your attention. Turn off the TV or smart phone when she wants to talk. Listen as if she is the most important thing in your life. *She is!*

+ Ask for her advice in every situation; do not make major decisions without her input and consideration.

+ Take time to notice her clothing, her hair, and little details that matter to her. Accentuate the positives. Take time to compliment her.

+ If household chores are stressing her out, ask her to make a list of things you can do to help. If she wants something done a certain way— loading the dishwasher or sorting laundry, for instance—try to do it that way. Many women are very particular about chores!

+ Initiate things that she likes to do. Make sure you *know* what she likes.

+ Show appreciation for her contributions, such as taking care of the kids, giving you advice, or her career. Be appreciative and say thank you.

+ Respect her monthly cycle or the change of life with kindness, understanding, protection, and lots of affection.

- Be gentle with lots of daily touches.

- Put her needs first in lovemaking. This requires *time* and an orgasm for her.

- Remember she is your "assignment from the Lord."

- As the head of the household, don't let discussions escalate into arguments. Be the one to admit wrongdoing first. The fact is, both mates usually bear some of the responsibility, so *you* be the man and say, "I'm sorry," even when you may be a little unsure about what you did to upset her. If she's upset, you need to make things right.

- Lead spiritually. Pray with her and pray with the children.

9

WHAT MEN WANT FROM WOMEN

By Gary Keesee

It is an honor for me to write this chapter. Although I do not claim to be an expert on male/female relationships, I have been married to Drenda, a female, for over thirty-eight years now. Secondly, as a male, I have some insight on the topic. So, ladies, grab your cup of coffee, get comfortable with a nice warm robe and some fuzzy slippers, and let's get started.

Oh, since I mentioned warm robes and fuzzy slippers, I might as well jump right into the slipper dilemma at our house.

HE'LL PASS ON ROBES AND SLIPPERS

If you came to our house, you would find a decent selection of soft robes and fuzzy slippers in my closet. What you would not see? Me wearing those things.

You see, Drenda absolutely loves warm fuzzy robes and slippers. I am convinced that to her, they are more important than food. I am not kidding. She always has a pair of slippers next to her bed and you will never see Drenda walking through the house without her slippers on—ever! I am convinced that if for some reason, her slippers were not found next to her bed in the morning and no one was there to bring them to her, she might starve to death.

She never takes a trip without packing them in her luggage either! When booking a hotel room, she will always ask if the room has a robe and slippers. So when she is looking for that perfect gift for her man, of course what could be better than a nice pair of slippers or a new robe, right?

I am guilty of making the same assumptions! In this super romantic brain of mine, when we were first married, I thought a great Christmas gift for my beautiful wife was a new pair of underwear—oh, sorry, ladies, I meant *panties*. I am sure you can guess how that went over. I also once bought her a vacuum cleaner for her birthday. Yikes, right?

Please don't misunderstand me, I love that she loves robes and slippers and I will buy them for her endlessly. You see, Drenda loves fashion; even at home with her robes and slippers, she is always in love with the colors, the fabric, and how she looks. I love that about her. She is so detailed and takes the time to make things beautiful, including herself. When I walk beside her, I feel like a king and am always admiring her beauty. The point I am making is that we are all different and unless we take the time to understand our differences, we will miss the benefit and the beauty that those differences bring into the relationship.

I would still be driving in circles somewhere if Drenda did not remind me when to turn. When it comes to directions, I can get lost in my own house. Well, not quite that bad but almost. Drenda is never lost! You can spin her around until she is so dizzy she is about to fall over, but when she stops spinning, she can still point you in the right direction every time.

I am glad that I have learned a few things over the years about Drenda and about women in general, but the bottom line is that we are different from each other. No matter what the media says about it, we are different—very different! When we take the time to understand each other's differences, we can appreciate what makes us different instead of attacking it.

WHEN WE TAKE THE TIME TO UNDERSTAND EACH OTHER'S DIFFERENCES, WE CAN APPRECIATE WHAT MAKES US DIFFERENT INSTEAD OF ATTACKING IT.

My parents built our home on my grandfather's farm in the country. Our house was about a quarter mile away from the farm, where I kept my pony, Tony. (See what I did there?) As a fourth grader, Tony was my transportation. We would ride out together in the summer, lazily soaking in the warmth and solitude of the open fields.

One day as I was riding, I glanced down and saw a four-leaf clover. I was amazed and overjoyed. It was like I had discovered a treasure. I had never seen one before, even though I had searched for one for years as I rode through the fields. I immediately stopped and picked it. I took it straight home and put it between two pages in an old book that I had to preserve it. To this day, I still have that book with the four-leaf clover in it. You see, I did not stop to pick one of the thousands of common three-leaf clovers that I passed every day, but rather it was the unique four-leaf clover that caught my attention.

And so it is in life. Our strength really *is* in our differences, our uniqueness, yet we spend so much time trying to be like everyone else, or trying to make our spouse just like us.

Unfortunately, the culture today is trying to make us believe that the difference between men and women does not exist! But no one is fooled. We all know we are different; we think differently and act differently because we *are* different. But that is where the beauty is. This is the great mystery... yet at the same time, this is the greatest victory. I do not need two of me; I already have my opinions and personal viewpoints. What I need is a completely different perspective, someone who has differing talents and abilities, someone who thinks differently than myself.

MEN WANT *EVERYTHING* FROM WOMEN

So, what do men want from women? That is an easy answer: everything that women are!

I should probably rephrase that question to, "What do men *need* from women?" But I won't because if men can understand what a woman brings into his life, he would embrace all of it. I will admit that my answer is a very broad one and I will try to break it down for you ladies as I go through this chapter. I hope.

Let me give you an example of what I learned from living with a woman.

We were building our new home in the country, doing much of the work ourselves. Drenda was the general contractor, working with scheduling the subcontractors while I ran our business and brought the money in to pay for it. Drenda is very gifted in many areas, but one of her strong points is seeing detail. On one particular day, the front steps were being poured. Our driveway is about nine hundred feet long and as we pulled in, Drenda kind of gasped when she saw the newly poured steps for the first time. She said, "Oh, no, those steps they poured are not level."

I thought, *What are you talking about? We are nine hundred feet from the steps and I can barely even see them from here.* I said, "What do you mean, they are not level?"

"I am telling you, those steps are off," she insisted.

I could not see anything that indicated they were off. They looked great to me. But Drenda assured me that the steps were lower on the right side compared to the left. I was convinced that they were not off—and if they *were*, there was no way she could tell from nine hundred feet away.

Well, we got into a little discussion about this. Not an argument, but a little discussion. So when we pulled up to the house, she insisted that I get a measuring tape, as I still could not tell if the steps were off. After measuring, sure enough, the right side was half an inch lower than the left side. I stood there in disbelief. Humbled again.

It ended up not being a problem because we were putting brick over the concrete-poured steps and that imbalance was easily taken care of. But the point I am making is that she *saw* something that I did not, incredible as it seemed to me.

This is the story of my life as a man. Drenda is usually right. Not all the time, but usually. It took me a few years of marriage to get a proper perspective about my wife's ability. In the early years, I viewed her attention to detail and opinions as a threat to my abilities, not understanding the awesome potential that I had with her on my team. Eventually, however, I got it. I thought, *Wait a minute, I did not see that the front steps were a half inch off but she did!*

This is a very small example of our differences, but Drenda has saved me from so many disasters and created so many solutions to what seemed like impossible situations that I will always thank God for her, acknowledging her as my true partner in all that we do.

Together, Drenda and I have created multimillion-dollar companies, built a flourishing church of thousands, created and launched two daily TV programs that are seen daily in every time zone in the world, and raised five awesome kids who all work for us and still say we are their favorite people to hang around with. I will admit that Drenda and I stay overwhelmed with what we have seen in our lives. Of course, knowing God and living life with His help and an understanding of His kingdom has been the defining factor in our success story. But if I were to rate what influences enabled our success outside of God's help, Drenda would be at the top. Of course, she is my help from God.

The Bible clearly says, "*He who finds a wife finds what is good and **receives favor** from the* LORD" (Proverbs 18:22).

So what is the *good* that a man receives that God calls *receiving favor* from Him? Basically, a man receives help! In other words, he is going to do better with both of them working together as a team rather than just working by himself. Unfortunately, so many men just do not get it. I have sat down with some very sharp ladies and yet their husbands are not prospering to the degree that they could be because the husband is not tapping into his teammate's awesome ability.

So let me give all of you ladies some encouragement: speak up! Do not be afraid to say something. Your husband needs your input. Your boss and workplace need your input. Men need your input. They need your wisdom and your perspective.

SPEAK UP, LADIES! DO NOT BE AFRAID TO SAY SOMETHING.
MEN NEED YOUR INPUT, YOUR WISDOM, AND YOUR PERSPECTIVE.

From my observations, however, some men are just not listening. So let me bring you into a man's world for a minute. If you want him to hear you when you speak, you must speak his language. I know that what I am about to tell you may not make sense, but trust me, it does to men and that is why you are reading this book, right? Also, please promise me you will hear me out before you make a quick judgment about what I am about to say. You see, ladies, a man's world is completely different from a woman's world.

THE #1 THING MEN WANT

First of all, let me say that what you see in Hollywood is not really what men want. Shocked? I hope so.

The picture of sex-crazed men, living a life of free sex—which does not exist, by the way—using anyone and everyone to get what they want is simply *not* what men want. Sure, there are some men who are living that way, but you would not want to end up as they usually do. So, let me just say it up front, the number one need of a man is *not* sex!

It is true that men need sex, as Drenda has pointed out. A man's body is constantly producing semen and that pressure releases hormones that drive him towards sex. And that sex drive is in your favor, ladies! God designed that drive to strengthen your marriage and your relationship and so much more, which I will talk about in a minute. But for now, I just want you to understand a man's greatest need is *not* sex. *It's respect!*

Did I hear a pin drop out there?

Yes, this is not what the mainstream Hollywood media puts out there, where a man is belittled and portrayed as a weak bystander in life. No, just the opposite. A man's world is one of respect and honor. It is this respect and honor that would cause a man to give his life to protect his family or go to war to protect his nation. So, ladies, it is vital that we have a discussion about the world of respect a man lives in.

A MAN'S WORLD IS ONE OF RESPECT AND HONOR.
IT CAUSES HIM TO GIVE HIS LIFE TO PROTECT HIS FAMILY OR GO TO WAR
TO PROTECT HIS NATION.

Let me give you an illustration of what I am talking about. If you listen to men talk when they first meet another man, you will most likely hear, "And what do you do for a living, Bill?"

Quite honestly, I have never heard a woman ask this as the lead-in to a conversation when they meet an unknown woman. Women will typically ask about the family or personal questions that revolve around relationship to begin a conversation. So why do men ask this question? It is all about respect. You see, in a man's world, his identity—who he is—is defined by what he does, his kingdom, which is what he owns and controls, and his woman.

Surprised by that last item?

Other men read a lot about a man when they meet his wife or female friend. Drenda and I found out a long time ago that if I am in a business situation, having her with me adds credibility and disarms suspicions. Of course, Drenda handles herself in a very business-like manner, in speech and appearance.

In a man's world, it is all about who he is. When a man asks another man what he does for a living, he is really determining how much respect or honor he should have toward this new guy he just met. He is trying to determine where this man fits in his world of respect. Ladies, you do a similar thing. I have watched women meet another woman and I have watched as their eyes go all the way to her feet and back up, looking at every detail. You are sizing each other up in your own way.

A man's world is typically always looking outward, from the present to the future, to conquer and build something, to achieve something, to win. Women are very much goal-oriented as well, but usually for different reasons. They see goals and winning as it relates to their family and relationships. A woman will ask, "How will this decision benefit those I love?" It is not that a man worships money or possessions, although they certainly can catch his attention if he is not careful. But rather, he has a natural bend towards achievement and competition. If you simply watch young boys play, it is always going to be about winning, competing, or building something. Now I am talking in generalities here, of course, but for the most part, this is true.

If you think back to your dating days, it was your admiration and interest in your husband's achievements that caught his attention. You may have said things like, "Wow, you are so strong" or complimented him on how great he did at something that met his need to be respected. Everyone knows that boys will show off for girls to gain their attention. This does not end with childhood. Men want to be admired and respected by their wives. If a man's wife is constantly finding fault with him, he'll look for admiration and respect from somewhere else. He might have an adulterous affair with a coworker not because she's prettier than his wife, but because she agreed with him, complimented him, or made an effort to help him on a project.

So, ladies, if you want to have a close relationship with your husband, your boss, or any man, you need to speak his language. As a woman, your natural language is one of affection and love, and this is your greatest need. And although men need love, their overwhelming desire is for *respect*.

Decision Analysts Inc. did a national survey on male-female relationships. One of the multiple choice questions it asked was:

Even the best relationships sometimes have conflicts on day-to-day issues. In the middle of a conflict with my wife/significant other, I am more likely to be feeling:

A. That my wife/significant other doesn't respect me right now.

B. That my wife/significant other doesn't love me right now.

Not surprisingly, 81.5 percent of men chose "A."[24]

I know what some of you ladies may be thinking. *Well, that is just ridiculous. You mean I can't even talk to my husband about the issues in our life without him feeling disrespected? Then what hope do I have?*

Hold on—this is what I have been trying to tell you. You must speak *his* language if you want him to hear you. When a man feels disrespected, he clams up and stops talking. Have you ever been there? I'm sure you have, and that's why what I am about to tell you is so important. As I said, men

24. For more, see Dr. Emerson Eggerichs, *Love & Respect: The Love She Most Desires, The Respect He Desperately Needs* (Nashville, TN: Thomas Nelson, 2004).

need your input and your wisdom, but they will never hear you if you do not speak their language.

WHY DO 81.5 PERCENT OF MEN FEEL DISRESPECTED IN A CONFLICT? USUALLY, IT'S BECAUSE A WOMAN IS TALKING TO HIM LIKE HE'S A FIRST-GRADER.

So what is going on if 81.5 percent of men feel disrespected in a conflict? If you stop and evaluate how you are talking to him, you might find your answer.

"You never do what I ask!"

"Why do you always…?"

"Why do I always have to take charge?"

"Why don't you ever *listen* to me?"

In other words, ask yourself if you are talking to him as if he was a first-grader.

I know you want me to hear *your* side of the story and I am sure there is one. But that is not the point here. I am trying to help you communicate with a man.

Let's imagine you are talking to your boss at work about an issue. Would you handle that any differently? (Please do not throw this book across the room.) Your husband is not your boss, of course, but he hears respect the same as your boss does. If you went into your boss's office and started complaining to him about this and that, putting him down, reminding him of all his weaknesses, I doubt you would have a job, right? So why would you think it would work with your husband or another man? It doesn't!

So instead of barking orders, offering insults, or making sarcastic remarks to the man in your life to get his attention, you might want to start your conversations with a real attention-getter: a compliment. Now, perhaps, you are thinking I am only saying this because I am a man and have *no idea* what I'm talking about.

Remember what I said about little boys showing off for the girls to get their attention? Have you seen how the boys perk up when the girls tell them how fast or strong they are?

In your world as a woman, communication is your tool of choice. You want to talk it out. Your goal is to strengthen the relationship by getting the issues on the table so things can be fixed. But as we learned, over 81 percent of men feel disrespected in a disagreement and almost all men will shut down communication in that environment.

Why do men shut down when they feel disrespected? Let's take a closer look into the man's world again. Men, typically, will back out of a situation instead of allowing it to escalate out of control if they respect the person they are talking to. So, ladies, in frustration, a man feeling overwhelmed will just back out, knowing that he cannot win a verbal argument with you.

It's important for you to understand this. Men *know* they cannot win in a verbal argument with women. When it comes to verbal combat, you are a black belt. You will just back up and repeat the same thing over and over until you feel he is hearing what you are saying. But he doesn't. He just shuts down.

You may be thinking, *Why doesn't he just say he is sorry or admit that he was wrong?* I agree he should and I coach men to do just that. But do you really want to verbally pin him to the ground and force him to say uncle? No one wins there. So again, there is a better way: you must learn to speak his language of respect.

Here is an experiment that will prove my point. The next time your husband is walking through the house, just yell out a compliment as he passes. "Hey, I really love how you…" and you can fill in the blank. It might be as simple as, "Hey, I love how you keep the car filled up with gas for me," or, "Hey, honey, the lawn looks great."

Here's what will happen: he will stop walking across the room and usually say, "What did you say?" Now, actually he heard you, but he will act like he didn't so he can hear it again. When you repeat it again, he will usually move closer to you with a different comment and this is where you insert your question or issue with a question. "Hey, I was wondering if you would have time to help me with something?" Or, "I have a problem that I need your insight on."

Do you see it? You are appealing to his language of respect. This is exactly how you would like your husband to talk to you, except your language is not a language of respect, it is a language of affection and love. If he yelled out to you as you walked through the room, "Man, I sure do love you. You are just an amazing mom and I appreciate all that you do for this family." You would stop and say, "What did you say?" He would repeat it and you would move closer to him. This is how it works!

The Bible teaches exactly what I have been telling you. Ephesians 5:33 says, *"Each one of you also must love his wife as he loves himself, and the wife must respect her husband."* Paul is commanding men to love and commanding women to respect. Why? Because speaking the language of love is not a man's natural language and the language of respect is not the normal language of a woman.

So, ladies, please keep a man's language in mind when you are talking to him. He needs you and he needs to hear that you respect him.

A MAN'S NEED FOR SEX

Now let's go on to the second thing a man needs, and that is sex. That is right, he needs it—God designed him that way for a good reason (which I'll get to in a second), although Satan loves to pervert that desire. This is not an option play for a man. If you take a look at the billions of dollars that are spent on porn, prostitution, and other sexual things, you will see just how much he has to have it and just how powerful his sex drive is.

As I have stated earlier, men are typically focused on goals and events, competition, job performance, business, and many other things. In a man's world, he can get so caught up in these things that he could possibly become a workaholic, emotionally leaving his wife and family out of the details of his life. And this would not be good for him and certainly not good for his wife's needs either. So God in His wisdom has given men a sex drive. Notice that word, *drive*. A man may start to wander emotionally from his relationship with his wife as he gets his identity from the outside world. But he is driven back toward his wife as she is the only one who has the legal right to relieve and satisfy that drive. Wise is the woman who understands this area of a man's life.

GOD IN HIS WISDOM GAVE MAN A SEX DRIVE TO DRIVE HIM INTO THE ARMS OF HIS WIFE.

Years ago, when Drenda and I were first married, sex was sometimes an awkward thing to talk about. We allowed strife and misunderstandings to rob us of the benefit of having sex many times. But I can remember the night that Drenda came home from church and apologized to me for allowing misunderstandings and the pressures we faced to interfere with our sex life. She said from that time forward, she would make love anytime I wanted to. Wow, what a relief. And she has held to that commitment ever since then.

As a woman, you may be afraid to grant such freedom to your husband. Maybe you're afraid he will take advantage of you. But this is where your faith comes into play. As you sow into your husband, trusting God, you are protecting your marriage from a strange woman. Secondly, you are giving your husband to God and allowing God to deal with his heart. And thirdly, there is an anointing on the sexual act once you are married. Because of that, I call it the oil of marriage.

A man has the obligation to meet your needs sexually as well as lay down his life for you, love you, and talk to you, to be romantic and affectionate toward you and meet your emotional needs as you are meeting his physical needs. Just remember that it takes time for both of us, men and women, to learn how to meet each other's needs. Someone has to be brave enough to sow as unto the Lord without concern of the response.

I remember one day I was really aggravated with Drenda. I do not remember what it was about, but I walked into my bedroom closet and prayed, "Lord, you have got to do something about Drenda. I am having a hard time with her." The second I said that, I heard His voice, which stopped me in my tracks. He said that Drenda was simply reflecting back to me the level of care and affection I was giving to her. If I wanted her to change, I needed to start sowing into her what she needed without any concern about her response. Well, I started doing that and I saw a huge change in our relationship.

In regard to sex, I absolutely do not advocate pornography in the home, masturbation, or any other means to short-circuit God's design for sexual union. However, I do want to bring you into a man's world for just a moment and help you as a wife protect your husband from this area of temptation.

As we have already said, men are visually stimulated—and porn is virtually everywhere. It should be no surprise to you that your man has probably seen porn somewhere in his life. In today's world of the Internet, many times, you can see it without even looking for it. Everything is online. Just doing a research paper can land you on a porn site. Since women are not typically motivated by sight, it may be hard to understand a man's dilemma.

LIKE A STARVING PERSON TEMPTED BY A PIECE OF CHOCOLATE CAKE, A MAN WHO HAS NOT HAD SEX FOR A WHILE MAY BE DRAWN TO PORN.

Let's say you have not eaten for two days and someone puts a piece of chocolate cake on the table in front of you. You know you should eat something more nutritious, but you are deeply tempted. This is what men feel like when they have not had sex for a while and they see porn. Defining "a while" is different for every man. It could be a couple of days or maybe a week before he needs sex again. Women tend to be shocked by this, but again, sex is a deep drive and hunger for men. This is why we see men do so many stupid things to get sex. Many times, they destroy their careers, their families, and their lives for it.

Let me be blunt: Drenda is my escape from sexual temptation. I do not have to be tempted by the chocolate cake because I can have some whenever I want.

In the same way men have to contend with sexual porn, women are often drawn to emotional porn that depicts a fairytale existence. My goal is that Drenda never has to imagine being emotionally fulfilled because she *is* fulfilled. Again, this takes open communication to reach this goal, but it is worth the effort. Drenda and I have an agreement that if I ever get caught off guard and see a picture that I should not have seen, I can come to her and confess that. This keeps my heart clean and our relationship pure. I tell men, "You will see images out there whether you want to or not. But the second glance is where you get in trouble. Guard your heart. Run from temptation."

THE THIRD THING MEN WANT

The third thing men need from women is friendship. Not the kind of friendship women have, where you may be sipping tea, laughing, and talking for hours. Yes, men absolutely need to take the time to talk to you. But men bond over action; the talking is secondary.

For years, when I took my boys fishing for the day, the first thing Drenda would say to me when I got home was, "What did you guys talk about?" To me, this was a very strange question. *What did we talk about? We were fishing!* I think I did say a couple of words to my sons, offering to move the boat a couple times, or asking if they were hungry. But all in all, we did not *talk*.

I know this is hard to comprehend, but men typically relate primarily by *doing* rather than talking. With this in mind, a man wants to *do* things with you. This is the way he relates. Drenda and I take cross-country motor-cycle rides, camping trips, and RV trips. We climb mountains and *do* all kinds of things. A man needs a buddy and he would prefer that this buddy be his wife, for sure. So be open to do new things and I believe you will find *doing* just as exciting as the men do.

ONE OF THE GREATEST THINGS MEN NEED

The list of what men need from women is longer than what I can cover here, but I have covered the main ones. But I believe this last one is proba-bly just as important as all the ones I have mentioned combined.

Then why did I not put it as the number one thing men need from women, you ask?

Because this one belongs in a category all by itself.

If I could title it, it might be that men need a spiritual referee. In a football game, the referee keeps the game moving according to the rules. If a violation occurs, he pulls out a yellow flag and throws it on the ground. This, for all intents and purposes, stops the game until the referees can confirm the foul, confront the player with what he did wrong, and then lay out the penalty for the error. They will even look at the instant replay film to make sure they have the call correct. Only after the foul has been identified and the proper penalty assessed can the game begin again.

A MAN NEEDS A WOMAN AS HIS SPIRITUAL REFEREE, TO LOVINGLY STOP THE GAME, SPEAK UP, AND CALL A FOUL WHEN ONE OCCURS.

Using this analogy, a man needs you to lovingly *stop the game*, speak up, and call the foul when you see it.

Drenda can tell when I am getting off of my spiritual game and she will call it every time.

I remember when we were looking for a building to rent to house our young church. The building we were in at the time was a radio station and we had outgrown it. The radio station was not charging us anything to meet there, which was awesome. Our church was in a very small town that had almost no commercial buildings where we could rent new space. Drenda went out and found a store was in the process of going out of business and they had a warehouse that would be coming available soon. The price was $4,000 a month. At the time, that seemed like a ton of money.

I hesitated to make a decision because although I knew we needed the building, I just could not get my head around spending $4,000 a month. Finally, I had procrastinated long enough; the owner said he needed to know *that day* if we were renting the building or not. As I sat in my office, I really had decided that we just could not afford such a monthly expense. Drenda came into the office and asked me what my decision was. I told her.

She did not agree; she thought it was a perfect place for our church. Finally, she said, "Have you prayed about this?" I had to be honest; I told her that I had not. Actually, I was afraid that God would say to go for it.

Drenda pulled out the referee flag and threw it to the ground. She said, "I am going to leave you here in your office. I want you to pray about it and then you come and tell me what God said. If you feel He said no to the building then I will submit to that. But you have to promise me you will at least pray about it."

Well, I agreed and started to pray. Not more than five minutes after I entered into prayer, I heard the Holy Spirit say, "Yes, this is your building."

This is only one of the many times Drenda has had to pull out the yellow flag and say in essence, "Stop the game; something is wrong." I love her for that and I need her to do that. In fact, every man needs that. So do not be afraid to pull the flag out or to call a timeout. God will show up.

I hope I have added some insight into a man's world for you. Like any topic, it would take an entire book to cover it well. To summarize what a man needs from a woman I will repeat what I said at the beginning of this chapter: a man needs *all of you!*

10

WHAT WOMEN WANT FROM MEN

WOMEN WANT LOVE

Guys, it probably goes without saying that women want *love* more than anything. The bigger question is, how do you show a woman that you love her? How often? How much?

For me, I'd say *incessantly*.

I once read that women need upwards of twenty affirmations a day to be happy. Those affirmations make us feel secure in the knowledge that we are loved. *We want to be loved and love the woman we have become.*[25]

More often than we care to admit, a woman's reflection of that love is filtered from the responses of others. A husband needs to speak words of praise toward his wife that evoke a sense of her being deeply loved. Yes, women must first of all love and respect themselves—but we do glean much of that reflection from others. Primarily, we want to feel that love and respect from the people in our life, first and foremost being our husband.

As women, we must learn to base our identity in who God says we are and His unfailing love for us since no man or woman can meet our needs

---

25. For more on this theme, see my book, *She Gets It: The 11 Lies that Hold Women Hostage* (Shippensburg, PA: Destiny Image, 2011).

entirely. The goal then, guys, is not to replace God for your wife, but to *represent Him* by affirming and encouraging her. Really, the golden rule solves most of our issues: *"Do to others what you would have them do to you"* (Matthew 7:12).

Actions and words—and lots of them—water the garden of love. Most women are looking for positive feedback about your feelings and admiration of them in a multifaceted, surprising, shock-and-awe menagerie of fireworks to unite them to you in holy love and bliss.

Okay, guys, I hope I haven't lost you there. My point is, women need love as much as you need respect. But for us, love is a big package that includes a myriad of gifts, not just respect, but also admiration and appreciation, *feeling wanted and needed.*

Want to make your wife happy? Give her details! Give her daily words of encouragement, find a new way to honor her different qualities, and note her accomplishments, your feelings for her, and how you do not ever want to be without her. And *then* say, "I love you." Your words and romantic actions are affirmations that she is loved and if you don't show her consistently, she will tend to doubt it.

YOUR WORDS AND ROMANTIC ACTIONS ARE AFFIRMATIONS THAT SHE IS LOVED AND IF YOU DON'T SHOW HER CONSISTENTLY, SHE WILL TEND TO DOUBT IT.

As love matures, don't take for granted that she chose this life with you. And, ladies, don't forget he chose the same. Gary and I share something we could never share with another: almost forty years of marriage, child-rearing, business-building, ministry-anointing, problem-solving, tear-comforting, and joy-celebrating. Although we get frustrated occasionally with one another, how could we ever say goodbye to the best and the most challenging life journeys shared in this holy commitment called marriage?

One night, I was feeling blue and told Gary that I felt we had gotten so busy, we were forgetting to be deep lovers. After a discussion, we both agreed that everything flows from our marriage and it was our highest priority. People come and go, popularity rises and falls, children grow and move out, but our marriage is lifelong.

Suddenly, Gary said, "Do you want to hear a hundred reasons why I love you?"

I was a bit shocked and yet delighted at the thought. I smiled. "I don't think you could make it to a hundred," I told him, "but give it a try!"

He began. He had me laughing and even crying, but he made it all the way to a hundred. I was thrilled. It was like a year's worth of affirmations in one night. I only wish I had recorded it because then I could have listened to it for the rest of our lives. I told Gary this and he said he was glad I didn't because I still need him. Of course I do! But that night ranks up there as one of the highlights of our marriage. It only cost him time and heartfelt creativity.

Give it a try with *your* wife. Use adjectives. "Pretty sparkling eyes that make me melt" is better than "I like your eyes," but start wherever you can.

> *Husbands, love your wives, just as Christ loved the church and gave himself up for her to make her holy, cleansing her by the washing with water through the word, and to present her to himself as a radiant church, without stain or wrinkle or any other blemish, but holy and blameless. In this same way, husbands ought to love their wives as their own bodies. He who loves his wife loves himself. After all, no one ever hated their own body, but they feed and care for their body, just as Christ does the church—for we are members of his body. "For this reason a man will leave his father and mother and be united to his wife, and the two will become one flesh." This is a profound mystery—but I am talking about Christ and the church. However, each one of you also must love his wife as he loves himself, and the wife must respect her husband.* (Ephesians 5:25–33)

WOMEN WANT RESPECT

Without apology, I have to say I'm a leader and have been since I was a bossy little girl telling my younger brother what to do and when to do it. It goes with the territory of being firstborn and coming from some independent boss girl stock. My great-aunt drove her husband around. My mother tells my father what to do hourly. (He would say more often.) I have had to learn my limitations the hard way, as well as when to lead a project or take charge, and when I am Gary's wife, not his boss. I've also struggled at times when I *should* take charge, but don't want to. It's always easier to tell someone else what they should be doing instead of doing what *we* should be doing! I've learned that not only does my husband not need a boss for a wife, I don't want to be his boss or cultivate a marriage where I need to be the boss because I trained him to follow me, instead of lead.

With that said, I was always the smart, studious girl at school and that was where I felt most confident. When Gary and I married, it was not on his list to value me for my knowledge. He'd say, "You're pretty," or "You're cute," or "You're funny" but he would never say, "You're really smart." So if he told me, "You're pretty," I would say, "Why do you never tell me I'm smart?"

I wasn't as smart as I thought to even say that!

What I was really saying was, "I want you to value me as a co-equal, a contributor to the vision and answers we need in life." I didn't want to be disrespected as someone who was *just a wife*. I'm sure I had also been trained by the feminist movement to think of that as a demeaning role. But honestly, I was really seeking the dynamic that God created for men and women: I truly wanted to be by his side and create a masterpiece together signed Gary and Drenda.

> *Husbands… be considerate as you live with your wives, and treat them with respect as the [physically] weaker [more delicate] partner and as heirs with you of the gracious gift of life, so that nothing will hinder your prayers.* (1 Peter 3:7)

Women want to be respected, treated as close confidants, and thanked for their contribution to problem-solving, not demeaned or taken for granted. We are looking to add value, to help the vision get there. We want to know that you see our effort, sacrifices, and contributions. This is also tied to feeling loved, to feeling valued, needed, and appreciated.

In the earlier days of our marriage, I often gave Gary perspectives, support, or advice to help him succeed, but he did not always give me a feeling of appreciation or credit in return. This caused some intense conflict a few times. I was more than glad to help him in any way. I would go to the ends of the earth to his aid—and I have—but I just wanted him to praise me in the city gates like the Scripture says!

Gary eventually confided in me that he struggled to give me credit at times because he thought it made him look like less of a man or incapable in my eyes. Reflecting on the way his father raised him, Gary thought that as a man, he should have all the answers.

In the early 1970s, Gary's father, Tom, took credit for the success of the business that his wife found and encouraged him to buy. He could never say, "I have built a great business, but it was Margie who found it and gave me the courage to go for it. I could have never done it without her!" Consequently, it left her to tell her side of the story when the success of their business was discussed. I always thought, *Why couldn't they tell the positive contributions of the other person and reward both of their successes and wonderful contribution? It truly was both of them contributing that made it happen.*

I spent more than a year doing research and leading our first church building program, but when the opportunity arose, Gary clearly failed to mention me at a meeting while thanking everyone else who had a part. I left feeling completely overlooked and unsatisfied. Everyone wants to be appreciated. I put in all the work for Gary and for God. I didn't really *need* to be thanked, but I wanted Gary to see my effort and reward it with his notice. *"All hard work brings a profit, but mere talk leads only to poverty"* (Proverbs 14:23). I wanted my work to be respected, not assumed or taken for granted. When I kindly confronted him with the fact that others were thanked, he apologized to me and said, "You're right. I should have thanked you as I did the others who contributed even less."

I didn't need to make it a huge ordeal. I *did* need to tell him my feelings.

ANY WOMAN—YOUR WIFE, AN EMPLOYEE, OR YOUR DAUGHTER—
STILL NEEDS TO HEAR "WELL DONE."

My point is this, guys: just because she may be your wife, an employee, or a daughter who has helped you for twenty years, she still needs to hear "well done." And in the workplace, if you fail to give honor where it is due, others will not respect her contribution as well. Wrong-hearted people may even disrespect her in such a way that she becomes fodder for gossip. I once heard a minister say that the best way to respect him was to respect his wife and children because they had paid a price equal to the one he had, if not more, because their roles were usually overlooked.

Conversely to offering words of appreciation, any negative words of humiliation, shame, or public embarrassment are devastating to a woman because they seriously subtract from the approval she desires to have from her husband and family. She will see it as rejection and surmise that she is unloved. Her deepest devotion is to you and her family; to feel she has failed at securing their love is almost unbearable. If this happens, out of survival, she may harden her heart and turn toward other persons or her career for the affirmation and love she seeks. Even worse, she may call it quits on you.

Make a decision that your wife will never want for love or encouragement from you. She will reciprocate with more than you give. Her heart will respond to your words, you will wash away the daily difficulties, and you will become the best of friends.

Just like guys, women need respect, but we want to *feel* it with "thank-yous" and share in the reward of spending the financial gain. Give your wife her reward and praise her in the city gates. (See Proverbs 31.)

WOMEN WANT PROVISION AND SECURITY

Provide purses for yourselves that will not wear out, a treasure in heaven that will never fail, where no thief comes near and no moth destroys. (Luke 12:33)

That is what we desire, the security of provision that doesn't run out. The tremendous pressure to buy things can quickly result in debt, which steals dreams and hopes with its strangling grip. What was a life of excitement can quickly become a pressure-filled existence doing something that one never wanted to do to pay for something that is no longer of value. God is the only answer to our need for provision and the sooner humility is applied to the situation and God brought on the scene, the better!

Within five years after we married, Gary and I were in a boatload of debt. Gary calls it *the five-year path to slavery*. We weren't frivolous; we just lacked wisdom and lived on commissions. Gary had to learn business coming from extreme shyness and uneasiness when meeting new people. There was a learning curve and our finances lagged behind our knowledge. We had so much debt and so little to show for it.

At our lowest point, Gary cried out to God, and heard the words, "You've trusted in debt more than you've trusted Me. You've never taken the time to find out how My Kingdom operates." Gary came to me and said, "I repented to God for relying on debt to meet our needs. I am going to learn how His Kingdom operates. I want to repent to you, too." That was the change in our life that began everything.

I have the greatest respect and admiration for Gary's humility and demonstrated leadership. He followed through and learned principles that were revolutionary to our lives and the lives of hundreds of thousands of others. It didn't change overnight, but we made it a pursuit together to find the biblical and practical answers and walk them out together. They worked. We found that when we approached God as a couple in unity, His promises became our answers and created a purse for us that has not worn out. We paid off the debts and began to live with a vision for our finances honoring God first. And He honored us. If you need financial help, get it! We have many resources and can produce a plan to give you hope and direction without charge.[26] We promised God that if He showed us how to be free ourselves, we would spend our lives helping others to find freedom. Our destiny together was tied to discovering how to work together and *fix the money thing*.

WHEN YOU HAVE THE HUMILITY TO ASK FOR HELP FROM GOD AND OTHERS, WOMEN SEE THAT AS A STRENGTH, NOT A WEAKNESS.

Your wife or female coworker wants to know you have the humility to ask for help from God and others. Women don't see that as weakness; we

---

26. Get started at forwardfinancialgroup.com.

see it as strength! But we also admire that you take charge of the direction of the family, company, or wherever your influence is when you are following a deeply held conviction. If you are the leader, lead. We will follow if you are committed to God and the vision. Women want to be led by someone who is following God and acting out of humility and meekness instead of domination.

Your wife knows you can't do this alone and she doesn't expect you to. It doesn't make you less of a man to need her help or God's. It affirms a deep sense of security in a woman that her husband is following his head, so she can struggle less to follow hers. It brings order and security to a chaotic world and peace to all fears of financial instability. Pray and seek God with your wife. Let her know what you are sensing and she will respect you even more! Share your vision with her and get her contribution and thoughts. Listen to her insights and point of view, too. She will be willing to sacrifice personal wants if she knows you have a vision.

Gary and I developed a shared mission and executed it as a couple. When I began to feel sorry for myself for doing without something, I reminded myself how great it would be to enjoy financial freedom. This helped me to stay disciplined. I also saw my husband doing everything in his power to carry out his part. Together, we did the impossible. This is the reward for discussing provision and the vision that will get you there as a team.

WOMEN WANT TO HAVE FUN

When I see photos of women from the 1940s and fifties sitting in lounge chairs, playing cards, or enjoying yard games with their children, I have to think we've missed something. Yes, I know we have so many choices, we can *be* anything, and *do* anything, but as my elementary school teacher drove into my training, "There is no freedom without responsibility!" Conversely, with all of the responsibility, there is also a loss of free time. Women have *no* time because we have taken on too many of the responsibilities of life, many of which used to belong to—or at least were shared by—men.

Oh, yes, it's grand that we can choose *anything* with our life. *But at their core, women are still girls.* Girls need fun and family, but women forget how to take the time for either. Girls don't continue to bear stress and pressure constantly without forgetting how to be free from worry and mental cognition that someone may need something from them at every waking moment of the day or night. Women are trying to work all day and often handle tearful or sick children at night. We need a break! Men often feel energized by their careers, but women get refueled during down time with their husband, family, and friends. It's just like that old Cyndi Lauper song, "Girls Just Want to Have Fun."

WOMEN WANT PROTECTION AND FREEDOM

To me, nothing says "I love you" more than Gary planning a night together apart from life's demands. Even though our nest is empty, the needs of our business and ministry life are constant. I need more than being his working partner; I need to be his wife. It's easy for him to forget this since I'm a strong woman and it looks like I can handle the pressure. But what we have both learned is that although I can run right alongside him at a full sprint in work, and sometimes will keep going like the Energizer Bunny, if I sprint for a few months without a break, I can fall apart. I want to be tough, but the fact is I'm still a girl who wants to play yard games with my kids, lie in a lounge chair at the beach, or snorkel with my grandkids. I am not invincible. I have to recharge. Women need to know that there is someone protecting them spiritually, emotionally, and physically. Yes, we bear responsibility for our choices, but love protects—and a man who protects us becomes a hero. Women still want heroes!

BY NATURE AND TO OUR OWN HARM,
WOMEN TEND TO BURN THE CANDLE AT BOTH ENDS.

By nature and to our own harm, women tend to burn the candle at both ends. I will work until I drop unless Gary protects me from myself! Occasionally, I have to remind him, "I'm not one of the guys and I really need a date night." And then I need him to remind *me* to not let it turn into work. I wouldn't trade anything for the opportunity to build dreams and businesses with my husband, but I *would* like to take a night off or a vacation—and I need him to save me from myself by planning one!

If a bad guy tried to bother me, I would want and expect Gary to step up and take him down. I believe in chivalry. Yet it's not bad guys who drag most women down, but the emotional stress of being responsible for so much.

More than 80 percent of women pay the bills without their husbands. Just because we *can* do it doesn't mean we *should*. When women pay the bills alone, they internalize the responsibility and stress. Unfortunately, some of that stress is released on the people they love the most.

It's not healthy for one person in the relationship to carry all the responsibility or the other person to not understand the reasons to work harder or budget financially. It can create divisions and a tug of war about money and how it's spent. If we are going to possess our dreams as a power couple, we must communicate about financial resources, which play into all decisions, from common vision and spending to saving and investing. We both need to be abreast of the facts and work together.

For me, it's best if Gary bears the heaviest part of this responsibility. I became a much happier woman when I let go of bill paying after our first years of marriage. Guys, if your wife has been doing the bills, change it and pay bills together when you are in a good mood, fed, and well-cared for. It will alleviate stress like nobody's business.

YOU NEED A CONSISTENT CONVERSATION ABOUT VISION AND BIG DECISIONS, A TIME TO DREAM AND TALK ABOUT FINANCIAL GOALS.

If money isn't tight and there's someone handling the bookkeeping, you still need a consistent conversation about vision and big decisions, a time to dream and talk about financial goals. This is more than bookkeeping; it's a once-a-month vision session to see where you are, how far you've come toward your ninety-day goals, and what adjustments need to be made. We have developed a habit of setting ninety-day goals toward bigger annual goals. This will keep you from aimlessly running the rat race without a focused destination of where you are going. It will also keep you from heading into two totally different directions that could destroy your relationship. Assess every ninety days how far you've come and reset your next ninety days. Reward your teamwork.

Share your vision and goals, hear hers, and then formulate a plan together. She wants to hear your heart and dreams, so share them and then let her fill in what she sees. The *how* can then begin to formulate in you both. Where there is no vision, people perish, and so do marriages, businesses, ministries, and families. Create vision together and then sit back in a lounge chair or play some yard games to reward yourself along the way! Freedom to decide your destiny and pursue it as a couple and family is more valuable than anything you will ever own.

WOMEN WANT TO FEEL UNDERSTOOD

Guys, this may be hard to fathom, but sometimes, women just don't know what's bothering them. It's true! There are times we as women don't get ourselves. We all have ups and downs in life. Usually, it's relational in some way—concern over a child, relative, or friend, or feelings of personal inadequacy. It can be feelings we can't explain or hurt feelings from a friend or foe. It could be hormonal changes, or a sudden memory of life's disappointments. And we burst into tears or start banging things around in the kitchen.

In these times, we need an understanding ear, a big-hearted hug and a kiss, or a neck rub. We need guys to speak respectfully, honor us, and refrain from using a tone of voice or volume that is frightening, demeaning, or sarcastic.

Consider your wife's feelings and wishes as a co-heir, one who receives an inheritance equal to yours. Loving your wife means you lay down your life for her, cherishing her, and esteeming her above yourself. Yes, this is a tall order, but the Holy Spirit in you is able to give you understanding and grace. Women who love God will respond with love and appreciation, ready to help you in any way they can.

Two are better than one, because they have a good return for their labor: if either of them falls down, one can help the other up. But pity anyone who falls and has no one to help them up. Also, if two lie down together, they will keep warm. But how can one keep warm alone? Though one may be overpowered, two can defend themselves. A cord of three strands is not quickly broken. (Ecclesiastes 4:9–12)

The *"cord of three strands"* symbolizes the joining of one man, one woman, and God into a marriage relationship. By keeping God at the center of your marriage, His love will bind you throughout your life together.

Obviously, men and women both have needs and hurts we should be sensitive to as well. Lack of understanding and consideration for one another can create a riff that actually affects God's response to our prayers. The Bible explains why a man's prayers aren't answered:

You ask, "Why?" It is because the LORD *is the witness between you and the wife of your youth. You have been unfaithful to her, though she is your partner, the wife of your marriage covenant. Has not the one God made you? You belong to him in body and spirit. And what does the one God seek? Godly offspring. So be on your guard, and do not be unfaithful to the wife of your youth. "The man who hates and divorces his wife," says the* LORD, *the God of Israel, "does violence to the one he should protect," says the* LORD *Almighty.* (Malachi 2:14–16)

Lack of forgiveness will hinder our faith from operating, but God says if a man acts treacherously toward his wife, God will act as a witness between them. In other words, God sees how you treat your wife in private, whether anyone else does or not. To act harshly with her or be unfaithful puts a man at odds with God. This includes adultery, pornography, abuse, or any betrayal.

There was once a woman who called Gary for financial counsel. She said, "Please don't tell my husband that I called or he will be mad and beat me." What?! The man was a church elder! Help us, Jesus! The truth is, this man did not have a relationship with Jesus; he had religion only. Gary turned to me angrily and said, "Some men need to be beaten!" That's how God feels about His daughters. Don't deal treacherously with your wife. She is God's primary concern and as you treat her, He will favor your life by answering your prayers. It's not too late to change.

Bitterness and lack of forgiveness toward one another creates division and strife, opening the door to the curse operating once again in your life, relationships, and finances. How's your marriage doing? It's a direct reflection of how well *you* are doing in other areas. If you want to prosper, be considerate and refuse to let anything come between you. Talk it out! That's why you must not let the sun go down on your anger. Don't carry it overnight or even a day. Be considerate and patient; build trust and understanding. You will prosper beyond your dreams.

A NOTE TO WOMEN

Maybe you have some other items on your wish list of what you want from your husband or men in general. This is a platform to begin discussing your personal needs and desires in your relationship and what's important to you. Whatever your wishes are, I hope you keep in mind that we can't expect these things while demanding control and treating our spouse, male coworkers, or any other guys in our life with contempt and anger. We can't have our cake and eat it, too. We must trust and contribute. There is a trade-off in every relationship. Covenants are stronger because both people offer their best to the other and become stronger together. The other side of the coin is knowing each other's weaknesses and working to shore up that area. We all have them, so we need to help one another.

11

I FORGIVE YOU... AND ME

As you already know, my road with men started off rocky from a very young age. When I was just a little girl, a babysitter abused me and said he would kill my little brother if I told my parents. Throughout my childhood and early teens, brokenness, abuse, and heartbreak began to bury me, until I hated myself for not being good enough, and I hated men for their actions against me. I guess that's why the feminist movement was so appealing—it elevated me above men, making me feel better about myself *and* it felt like a way of paying back my abusers.

I know this story is nothing new to many who have been misused, taken advantage of, or neglected as a child. Many have experienced hurt that can't be dismissed by simply saying, "Move on." A lot of times, we talk about forgiveness like it's this perfectly wrapped present that's as easy as handing to our offender and walking away. However, in a lot of situations, forgiveness feels more like a 30,000-pound anchor that we're trying to pull up by hand from the bottom of the ocean.

That's the kind of forgiveness I want to talk about in this book because I have found that often, our issues with the opposite sex stem from deep-seated wounds, memories, and mindsets—things that have become so much a part of who we are, we no longer realize we are still dragging them around. We might wonder why we got so angry when our spouse left toothpaste on the sink, or forgot to take the trash out, or innocently said something we interpreted as a slight, but the answer often lies in our past—that 30,000-pound anchor that has kept our ship grounded for way too long.

I learned the hard way that the *only* person who stands to lose something when you hold on to bitterness and unforgiveness is you. When you plant your feet into unforgiveness, your life comes to a screeching halt. You begin to circle around that situation, never able to move forward, experience lasting joy, or live in true freedom.

I want to encourage you—God's grace is sufficient. It's not always easy to let go of those seeds of unforgiveness, but it *is* possible and it's so worth it! Jesus willingly gave His life for a world that hated Him, doubted Him, misjudged Him, tortured Him, lied about Him, and crucified Him. Love in its purest form looks a lot like forgiveness.

JESUS WILLINGLY GAVE HIS LIFE FOR A WORLD THAT HATED HIM,
TORTURED HIM, LIED ABOUT HIM, AND CRUCIFIED HIM.
LOVE IN ITS PUREST FORM LOOKS A LOT LIKE FORGIVENESS.

Have you ever met someone who blamed their life decisions on something that happened to them as a child? I have known people who've allowed a nasty comment that was said about them in their teens to prevent them from accomplishing anything in their fifties. I have seen people allow a bad situation with one job become an excuse to stop trying for the rest of their career. I have watched bitterness poison many people's lives, including my own.

When Gary and I were newlyweds, I projected all of my hurt and fears from men in my past onto our relationship. It was terrible! If Gary told me he loved me, I struggled to believe him. If he complimented me, I thought he wanted something. My mindset on love and men was totally skewed. Although I was a Christian, there were areas where I still hadn't let God's forgiveness wash over and cleanse me.

The horrible thing was, my unforgiveness toward the men in my past *wasn't* affecting them at all. Instead, it affected Gary, my sweet husband!

My unforgiveness towards things that happened years before, from early childhood, was now wreaking havoc in my marriage. Gary was paying the price for sins he had never committed against me.

My husband is a very calm man. He doesn't easily get upset or angry, but I'll never forget the altercation we had a few years into our marriage. I can't remember how it started, but I was upset. No matter how Gary tried to console me, I became angrier and more emotional. I yelled, "You don't love me! You don't love me!"

Gary was so frustrated that he started to laugh. He didn't know what to do! He had tried to say the nicest, most loving words to me, but nothing made me happy. If he said he loved me, I didn't believe him. If he said I was beautiful, I didn't believe him. I wanted him to fill something in me that couldn't be filled. I was looking for my identity in him instead of in God's love.

When he sighed with a frustrated laugh, I *lost* it. All of my insecurities shouted, "He's mocking you! He's making fun of you!" I went into a fit of rage, crying and slamming doors. I locked myself in our bathroom and refused to open the door. I guess I wanted him to bust it open and *prove* his love to me. Prove that I was worthy. Eventually, he surrendered and went to sleep. As I climbed into bed that night, I was determined to make his sleep as wretched as I felt. I tossed and turned, jabbed him with my elbow, and made every effort to show him how bothered I was.

I thought, *If I'm miserable*, he's *going to be miserable.*

I am ashamed to admit the extent to which I went in an effort to find approval. The next morning, I was still upset. Gary broke down in tears and said, "Drenda, I love you, but I don't know how I can get it through that thick wall and that thick head of yours and help you see how much I love you." The problem was in me, not him. Unforgiveness will affect every area of your life if you don't let it go.

UNFORGIVENESS WILL AFFECT EVERY AREA OF YOUR LIFE IF YOU DON'T LET IT GO.

Forgiving people for unintentional mistakes or hurtful words that were said in the heat of the moment can be tricky enough. It can be even harder to forgive another person's intentionally malicious actions, such as a broken heart, abuse, molestation, cheating, rejection, or abandonment. If you have been through one of those situations, you might be tempted to say, "I have the right to be angry about this—what they did was wrong!"

And you're right. It *was* wrong and it caused real pain. But holding on to it and letting it poison your life is really self-abuse. Forgiveness doesn't mean you are saying what people have done to you in the past was okay; it just means you're letting go of the hurt, letting God heal the situation, and letting yourself move on and experience God's joy again.

> To forgive is to set a prisoner free and discover that the prisoner was you. —Lewis B. Smedes

When we get emotionally hurt, it's almost like getting a splinter. As long as we protect that splinter and don't remove it, it won't heal. It continues to hurt and fester; it can even become infected, so that small splinter becomes a much bigger problem. Hurt is the same way. We have to stop protecting our hurt, rehearsing the bad things that have been done to us, and dwelling on the past. Otherwise, those hurts won't heal. We have to stop carrying our hurts and let God remove them from our lives.

Forgiveness is the answer. Jesus died on the cross to heal your broken heart and give you a fresh start. Jesus took the scars on His hands so you wouldn't have to carry the scars on your heart anymore. There is no circumstance too severe or difficult for God to restore and heal. If we truly believe that God restores, we know that nothing in our past can become an excuse or ceiling for our actions or what we can accomplish in the future. Forgiving someone doesn't mean what they did was right. It just means you're ready to be whole again.

FORGIVING SOMEONE DOESN'T MEAN WHAT THEY DID WAS RIGHT.
IT JUST MEANS YOU'RE READY TO BE WHOLE AGAIN.

Some people have told me, "I want to forgive them, but I just can't. I'm still so angry about it." Forgiveness may not immediately take away your emotions about the situation, but it's the first step. Forgiveness is like undergoing surgery; the issue is fixed, but healing still must take place afterward. Continue to make the daily choice to forgive until you no longer feel any resentment or bitterness toward the situation.

If you have been hurt by somebody of the opposite sex, whether in your distant past or more recently, I want to encourage you to pray this prayer today:

God, I give You my heartbreak, my disappointed expectations, and everything I have held against the people around me. I love You and I cast my cares on You. I forgive [the person's name] for what they did to me. What they did wasn't right, but I don't want to let unforgiveness keep me bound to my past. I'm letting go of that hurt today. Thank You for sending Jesus to set me free from heartbreak—I receive that today. Renew my joy and help me trust people again. Amen!

FORGIVING YOURSELF

One of the hardest people to forgive is often ourselves. I was seventeen when I had an abortion. I tried to bury the hurt. I was supposed to be *a strong woman*, the kind of woman who takes what she wants without worrying about how it affects other people. I had previously told a pregnant friend she should get an abortion, but when it was me, I felt ashamed. I didn't know why, but something in my deepest heart knew it wasn't right, so I hid it from my feminist friends and my family.

I acted like everything was fine when I was around people, but at home, I was thinking about ways I could take my life. The guilt and shame consumed me, so much so that I didn't know how I would go on with my life. I felt more unlovable than ever. It felt like a part of me died that day in the abortion clinic.

I soon found the miraculous love of God through a friend and life became much better... but still not perfect. I was still insecure. I still battled the feelings of guilt and shame from my past.

I'll never forget when I broke down into tears and told my pastor about the abortion. Every weekend, I heard that Jesus paid the price for my sins and I was free, but as a young woman new to Christ, my pastor's reaction was confusing to me. "God forgave you, Drenda," he began. He hesitated. "But don't tell anyone else in the church about it," he told me. "They might not understand and I don't want them to judge you."

Judge me? I felt like I had committed an unpardonable sin that was too bad for even the church to forgive.

Satan wants to discourage you to the point of giving up. He is out to destroy your life. He wants to make you feel unlovable and untalented, too far gone for God to ever love you. Satan knows if he can steal your identity in Christ, he can get you to believe lies about who you are and who you were created to be.

SATAN KNOWS IF HE CAN STEAL YOUR IDENTITY IN CHRIST, HE CAN GET YOU TO BELIEVE LIES ABOUT WHO YOU ARE AND WHO YOU WERE CREATED TO BE.

Growing up, I heard the critical words of family members who made me feel unworthy. At school, boys hurt me with *their* nasty remarks and female teachers told me the only way to win was to embrace the feminist movement and hurt men before they hurt you.

And now, here at church, my pastor was telling me that my sin was too great and I should hide it. I know he was trying to protect me, but talk about shame!

Our kids always loved to play Jenga while they were growing up. We'd build up the tower of little wooden blocks and then each take turns removing one, hoping not to shake the foundation too much until it came toppling down during someone's turn. As our family became better at the game, we all knew what pieces to grab first—the ones toward the top and middle. We learned that pulling out the Jenga pieces on the bottom few rows made the tower very unstable.

Our identity in Christ is like the bottom rows of a Jenga tower. Satan knows stealing our confidence gives him the best chance of knocking us down. When we let Satan jerk our chain with condemnation, guilt, and insecurity, he knows he can use that to get the rest of our life's tower to collapse—our relationships, our family life, our purpose, our joy, our passion, and so much more.

Unforgiveness toward yourself can grow into so much more than feeling bad about making a mistake, or being insecure about something. It's a deceptive snare the enemy wants to use to take you down. Unforgiveness is a deliberate *strategy* of the enemy. Don't bite the bait!

It's no coincidence that we hear lies that attack our identity and value every single day. Like me, many find themselves running into the arms of bad relationships, guilt, performing for approval, stress, overwhelming shame, and, ultimately, sin, as they try to escape from *themselves*. In today's culture, every norm has been challenged, and the result is a loss of identity in every way imaginable. The attack on self-worth is worse than an identity crisis; it's an identity takeover!

It doesn't help that on top of the guilt and pressure we put on ourselves from our mistakes, every day, an overwhelming amount of messaging and marketing is targeting every soul on the planet to sell us on the idea that we are missing something, that we're not enough. We think:

If I was prettier…

If I was handsome…

If I was skinnier…

If I was buff…

If I was smarter…

If I was richer…

If I had more curves…

If I was taller…

If I was shorter…

If I talked more…

If I talked less…

Are you noticing a pattern? There's no win! Satan wants to convince you that you aren't good enough. He is in a battle for your *mind*. He wants to lead you into temptation, and then beat you up with condemnation for making one mistake. If you listen to his lies, that nagging voice of insecurity, regret, and guilt will never stop hammering at you. The devil will *always* tell you that you're *too something* to be used by God.

One of the voices Satan often uses to make us feel inadequate is our culture—through media, magazines, social media, and advertisements. Do you know their little secret? Marketers aren't trying to make you feel *good*; they're trying to convince you that you have a problem that *they* can solve so they can pocket your money! Next time you see an ad, remember that it is a photoshopped image *designed* to make you feel like you are missing something. Companies don't make money when you feel content. That's why we have to learn to work *from* identity instead of *for* identity. We have to know who we are and what we have in Christ, so we know what we can *do* through Him!

> *Therefore, if anyone is in Christ, the new creation has come: The old has gone, the new is here!* (2 Corinthians 5:17)

If we use the culture as our mirror, we will always be unhappy, always falling short and chasing the world's cures to make us more lovable, more attractive, and more worthy... to no avail.

Fortunately, amidst a hostile culture that is bent on an identity takeover, God is still speaking. If we are trained, we can hear, "This is my son and daughter, in whom I am pleased." Not only does God have pleasure in us as His, but there also is pleasure for each of us in knowing our true identity, the way He sees us, apart from the voices that surround us.

For the record, *you* are worthy. *You* are worth loving. There is nothing you have done in your past, or anything that you are missing, that disqualifies you from the love of God. God has a *good* plan for your life!

After I had an abortion, I wondered if God could ever use me. I felt like I had blown it too much for anyone to forgive me—even God. I was *so* wrong. God showed me that Jesus knew all about my mistakes before He went to the cross, but He still chose to do that for *me*. Me! He was thinking of me, and how much He loves me. Guess what? He was thinking of you, too! God has done a work in my life that's beyond anything I could have ever asked for, thought, or imagined—and He wants to do the same for you. No matter what you've done, it's not too late.

If we confess our sins, he is faithful and just and will forgive us our sins and purify us from all unrighteousness.   (1 John 1:9)

If you have been harboring unforgiveness toward yourself, I want to challenge you to pray this prayer out loud today and really take every word to heart:

God, I am in awe of Your love. You forgave me for my mistakes 2,000 years ago, and You said nothing could separate me from You. Today, I am choosing to forgive myself the same way You already forgave me. Please, help to bring restoration in this area of my life. Help me to keep my eyes on who You say I am and not listen to the lies of the enemy. I love You, and I want to encounter Your love for me in an even greater way. I want to be used by You, God. Thank You so much for sending Your son to die for me. Amen!

12

TO MARRY OR NOT TO MARRY
(AND OTHER HARD QUESTIONS)

In God's plan for men and women, is it wrong to be single?

Is marriage out of style?

How should single men and women relate to each other and the world around them?

How do I prepare for marriage while single?

Does being single mean I am less valuable than married people? Do I have to be lonely?

Unfortunately, our culture often ridicules women for being women. It is no longer politically correct to even mention that you may want to have children someday—or, God forbid, stay with them as a stay-at-home mom. Women are encouraged to emulate men in the workplace and in life.

During a trip to Italy, I came across some really strange content about this very topic that involved *Vestal Virgins*, a cultish practice observed during the Roman Empire.

The thought occurred to me, *Had Jesus any knowledge of the Vestal Virgins when He shared the story of the ten virgins?* I prayed and couldn't let go of the thought. Jesus was so adept at sharing parables that would spiritually enlighten people within their culture. We often lose sight of this human side of Jesus, forgetting He was both God and man. Because He was God yet came to us as a man, He was able to bring God's truths to humans in a way that related to their lives. Hebrews 4:15 says, *"For we do not have a high priest who is unable to empathize with our weaknesses, but we have one who has been tempted in every way, just as we are—yet he did not sin."*

Who were the vestal Virgins of Rome, and did they impact ideas about Christianity? Do we see these attitudes toward women, motherhood, virginity, and leadership today?

THE VESTAL VIRGINS

The Vestal Virgins were a small group of women, typically six, who were chosen between the ages of six and ten years old. Their aristocrat fathers would offer them up for possible selection by the Roman Empire. This cult group took their name from Vesta, the goddess of hearth (i.e. fire) and home. Their duties included preparing sacrificial meals, keeping the temple fire lit, and collecting water from a sacred spring.

If selected, the virgin was required to take an oath to the state and a thirty-year vow of celibacy. In essence, these women were stripped of their birthright to reproduction. They were not released into society for possible marriage until they were forty or in their late thirties. One author notes:

> The Vestal Virgins are an example of a male-defined idealized womanhood, which disempowers women according to male social values.… They are taken out of society before they are women, as premenstrual girls of 6, and remain sexually inactive on pain of death. As "de-sexed" women they are then "safe" to be granted some powers that only men, the first gender in Roman society, can properly expect to exercise.[27]

The privileges granted to these priestesses of Vesta included places of honor at games and performances. However, they were severely punished if they broke their vow of celibacy, let the temple fire go out, or were accused of impropriety or misconduct. They could become scapegoats for

27. Deborah F. Sawyer, *Women and Religion in the First Christian Centuries* (New York: Routledge, 1996).

any misfortune. Punishment might include a beating or being left to die in an underground tomb.

ARE SINGLES HOLIER?

The early church embraced the idea of singleness as a means to holiness. Rather than trusting the atoning work of Christ for holiness, those who wished to follow Him fully were urged to refrain from marriage and take a vow of celibacy. This became mandatory for anyone entering ministry as clergy, whether monks, nuns, or priests.

Jerome of Stridon, a priest who died around 420 AD, wrote:

As long as woman is for birth and children, she is different from man as body is from soul. But if she wishes to serve Christ more than the world, then she will cease to be a woman and will be called man.[28]

Sound familiar?

In the late fourth century, Ambrose, the archbishop of Milan, wrote:

She who does not believe is a woman and should be designated by the name of her bodily sex, whereas she who believes progresses to complete manhood, to the measure of the adulthood of Christ. She then does without worldly name, gender of body, youthful seductiveness, and garrulousness of old age.[29]

These centuries-old ideas about womanhood now exist outside the church. Modern-day feminists put down women who choose marriage and motherhood, esteeming instead those who stay single. Interestingly, some women in the early church shaved their heads and dressed in masculine attire, although Paul and some other clergy denounced these practices.

I was a mere fifth grader when women started burning their bras in 1968, but I embraced the ideology of not wearing one throughout many of my school years until I could no longer pass the pencil test. (Ask your mom

---

28. Cheryl Glenn, *Rhetoric Retold: Regendering the Tradition from Antiquity Through the Renaissance* (Carbondale, IL: Southern Illinois University, 1997).
29. Ibid.

or grandma about this "test"!) Wearing a bra somehow made us too female. Rebellion never makes sense.

On one hand, modern society rejects the differences God gave the sexes and rebels against marriage, motherhood, and femininity. On the other hand, some religious traditions still promote celibacy as a path to holiness. All of this is madness.

Marriage and sex within marriage are *holy*. After all, God's first commandment to woman and man was to be fruitful and multiply. God orchestrated the first marriage and created sex for intimacy as beautifully displayed in the Song of Solomon. Likewise, singleness can also be holy. Paul made it clear that his singleness gave him the time and focus to preach the gospel. Anna the prophetess was a widow who served the early church faithfully.

Single persons have an opportunity to devote themselves to ministry, but God does not require them to be single. Whether rooted in feminism or religion, the spirit of error is at work in the world in an attempt to pervert the goodness of God, His creation, and our freedom in Christ. The Scriptures tell us, *"There is neither Jew nor Gentile, neither slave nor free, nor is there male and female, for you are all one in Christ Jesus"* (Galatians 3:28). Clearly, this means all of us can be holy.

I have counseled with those who are *afraid* of marriage or commitment because both secular and religious teachings have attacked the institution, lessened its importance, or overemphasized it to the point of judgment. Fear is not from God! The enemy comes to steal with his hissed, *"Did God really say…?"* He has plenty of schemes to throw at us, such as confusing sexual identity, placing women in desexualized roles or positions, or murdering our God-given desire to reproduce.

THE DEVIL HAS PLENTY OF SCHEMES TO THROW AT US,
SUCH AS CONFUSING SEXUAL IDENTITY, PLACING WOMEN IN DESEXUALIZED ROLES
OR POSITIONS, OR MURDERING OUR GOD-GIVEN DESIRE TO REPRODUCE.

Jesus came to give us life, not a lie. He is the only one who can help us navigate His plan for our lives. That plan won't violate His Word; it will help us fulfill it in His strength and the power of the Holy Spirit, the fuel for living in true holiness.

THE PARABLE OF THE TEN VIRGINS

Circling back to the beginning of this chapter, I think it's possible that Jesus chose to tell the story of the ten virgins to illustrate the importance of focusing on God and His Spirit. Jesus took a key part of the culture at that time and used it to point people to the kingdom of heaven. In stark contrast to the idolatry of the Vestal Virgins, I believe Jesus presented a beautiful picture of the ten virgins and the marriage supper to detail our responsibility to keep our heart lit with the fire of the Holy Spirit. Jesus is the coming Bridegroom and we must be ready for Him.

> *The kingdom of heaven will be like ten virgins who took their lamps and went out to meet the bridegroom. Five of them were foolish and five were wise. The foolish ones took their lamps but did not take any oil with them. The wise ones, however, took oil in jars along with their lamps. The bridegroom was a long time in coming, and they all became drowsy and fell asleep. At midnight the cry rang out: "Here's the bridegroom! Come out to meet him!" Then all the virgins woke up and trimmed their lamps. The foolish ones said to the wise, "Give us some of your oil; our lamps are going out." "No," they replied, "there may not be enough for both us and you. Instead, go to those who sell oil and buy some for yourselves." But while they were on their way to buy the oil, the bridegroom arrived. The virgins who were ready went in with him to the wedding banquet. And the door was shut. Later the others also came. "Lord, Lord," they said, "open the door for us!" But he replied, "Truly I tell you, I don't know you." Therefore keep watch, because you do not know the day or the hour.* (Matthew 25:1–13)

In this parable, the ten virgins are excitedly waiting for the groom and the wedding ceremony, but five of them are unprepared. We should be as ready as the five wise virgins and long for Christ as eagerly as they did.

Both marrying or living a chaste, single life are just as righteous, depending on the Holy Spirit's grace and direction on your life. Paul makes it clear that singleness is a gift. He wrote:

I wish that all of you were as I am. But each of you has your own gift from God; one has this gift, another has that. Now to the unmarried and the widows I say: It is good for them to stay unmarried, as I do. But if they cannot control themselves, they should marry, for it is better to marry than to burn with passion. (1 Corinthians 7:7–9)

The Scriptures clearly tell us that it is a sin to commit fornication (sex outside of marriage) or adultery (sex with someone other than your spouse). Jesus took it further and said, *"Anyone who looks at a woman lustfully has already committed adultery with her in his heart"* (Matthew 5:28). This would certainly include viewing pornography. Jesus made it clear that all sin emanates from desires in the heart. Religion is not about the heart, but focused on do's and don'ts that the human heart has a way of manipulating its way around for justification or gain.

GOD'S LIFE FOR US REQUIRES FAITH TO LEAN ON HIM, WHETHER MARRIED OR SINGLE.

God's life for us requires faith to lean on Him, whether married or single. If you are not called to a celibate life, pray and seek God for a marriage partner. The process of waiting, through faith and patience, will still require self-control, which will come in handy when you do marry. If God has given you the grace to remain single, go for it; otherwise, marriage is clearly the right course rather than to burn with lust. In either station, married or unmarried, sexual immorality violates God's command and His plan. Fornication, adultery, homosexuality, or any such forms of behavior sexually deviate from His truth.

Following Jesus is not a form of religion. In our culture, we *follow* people, but we also *unfollow* them on social media if they've offended us. We are not just to follow Jesus, but must also submit ourselves to His Lordship. He once asked his disciples, *"Why do you call me, 'Lord, Lord,' and do not do what I say?"* (Luke 6:46).

God never asks of us what He will not supply us the grace (His power) to accomplish and bring blessings with our obedience. He wants to give us a rich and satisfying life.

WHO SHOULD YOU MARRY?

If God has called you to marriage, He must also supply a suitable mate, just like He did for Adam and Eve. God will not violate His Word by giving you someone of the same sex as your marriage partner. (See Romans 1:18–32.) I have heard it said, "I will not love a God who will not let me choose to love who I want to love." God *is* love. If you love Him, wouldn't you love the mate He's chosen for you?

A *suitable* marriage is to someone who is also a believer in Christ. The Bible says:

> Do not be yoked together with unbelievers. For what do righteousness and wickedness have in common? Or what fellowship can light have with darkness? What harmony is there between Christ and Belial [the devil]? Or what does a believer have in common with an unbeliever? What agreement is there between the temple of God and idols? For we are the temple of the living God.   (2 Corinthians 6:14–16)

Thus, a suitable marriage partner is a single person of the opposite sex who loves Christ. Where is this person? Well, they are most likely *not* found during happy hour at some bar. I encourage you to pray and trust God as you serve Him faithfully, believing that He will cause you to cross paths with the love of your life. I am not suggesting a scouting trip where you desperately seek a mate like a football coach looking for a new pass rusher, or a fashionista shopping for a vintage handbag. But if you serve the Lord with all your heart and go where He is working, you will meet within His people someone who is also doing the same. Besides going to church on Sundays, think about mission's trips, feeding the hungry, volunteering on a team, conducting Bible studies, or helping children.

Seriously avoid single's traps, like bars and clubs where there are strong temptations to hook up, intoxicating deceptions to escape loneliness with a lack of accountability. God places the solitary in families (see Psalm 68:6) so spend time with the family of Christ, with married couples and families.

Learn, observe, and grow. Friendship is the best prerequisite for marriage, so start any relationship as friends with strong boundaries. Some of the best marriages result from meetings arranged by married Christian friends, who have more experience and know what you need to look for. First Timothy 5:2 admonishes us to treat older women as we would our own mothers *"and younger women as sisters, with absolute purity."*

FRIENDSHIP IS THE BEST PREREQUISITE FOR MARRIAGE, SO START ANY RELATIONSHIP AS FRIENDS WITH STRONG BOUNDARIES.

I'm often asked, "Is it wrong to use the Internet to meet people?" While God can use any means to bring a man and a woman together, be discreet, wise, and *slow* to move. Infatuation and a potentially exciting rendezvous can cloud your judgment. People are often not who they present themselves to be, especially sharks! *Time will tell* is still a wise admonition.

If you meet someone over the Internet, make sure they are a true believer; meet their pastor, church, and family members so you're sure it's not just a ruse. If they don't want you to meet them or something seems fishy, run fast! If everything seems okay, be slow to move forward and get the input of those you are accountable to spiritually. The right person will pass the test. Compromising and settling for the wrong person will only bring heartache. It's better to be single than unhappily involved or married.

As a young woman and then new believer, with little to no biblical training, I made several regrettable mistakes in relationships and hurt others in the process. *"The wages of sin is death"* (Romans 6:23). Death is ugly, but thank God, He brings life in the Spirit. I had to back up, receive forgiveness through the sacrifice of Jesus Christ, recognize my ways were wrong, and align my beliefs with God's Word. I was determined to get it right by the grace of God. After I made these choices, I met Gary.

The first time we met, I was trying so hard not to fall into a wrong relationship again that I was not open at all. I actually rebuked the thought of being with him when it came! Working together as friends over the course of the school year, I saw his love for God and grew to admire him, but was still somewhat afraid of making a mistake. We had normal ups and downs, as all friends do. The final determining factor for me was my pastor's confirmation that Gary was the right man for me. I had prayed for this confirmation and God gave it to me.

God is able to meet you where you are and give you the answers that you seek. Only first, you must seek!

WAITING FOR THE RIGHT ONE

I love the story of Rebekah at the well in Nahor. (See Genesis 24). Now obviously some things have changed, but the principles of this story have not. Abraham sent his servant, Eliezer, to find a suitable wife for his son with the prerequisite that she must come from *among those who shared his faith.* It was nearly evening when Eliezer arrived in town. He and his camels were thirsty.

> *Then he prayed, "LORD, God of my master Abraham, make me successful today, and show kindness to my master Abraham. See, I am standing beside this spring, and the daughters of the townspeople are coming out to draw water. May it be that when I say to a young woman, 'Please let down your jar that I may have a drink,' and she says, 'Drink, and I'll water your camels too'—let her be the one you have chosen for your servant Isaac. By this I will know that you have shown kindness to my master." Before he had finished praying, Rebekah came out with her jar on her shoulder. She was the daughter of Bethuel son of Milkah, who was the wife of Abraham's brother Nahor. The woman was very beautiful, a virgin; no man had ever slept with her. She went down to the spring, filled her jar and came up again.* (Genesis 24:12–16)

Let's stop here for a moment and note some principles: she was beautiful, so she cared for her appearance; she was a virgin, not promiscuous; and she was working, not bemoaning her singleness. We could suggest these same principles for men as well: care for your appearance; don't be sexually active; be content; and work. The Holy Spirit is watching the choices you make. You are qualifying yourself as marriageable in your choices to both trust God and serve faithfully.

THE HOLY SPIRIT IS WATCHING THE CHOICES YOU MAKE.
YOU ARE QUALIFYING YOURSELF AS MARRIAGEABLE IN YOUR CHOICES
TO BOTH TRUST GOD AND SERVE FAITHFULLY.

The servant hurried to meet her and said, "Please give me a little water from your jar." "Drink, my lord," she said, and quickly lowered the jar to her hands and gave him a drink. After she had given him a drink, she said, "I'll draw water for your camels too, until they have had enough to drink." (Genesis 24:17–19)

Here's another character principle: Rebekah went the extra mile! She didn't grumble about her job carrying water to her family, but she was extremely helpful before she saw any personal advantage for herself in serving this person. She wasn't a charmer, deceitful, or vain. She was helpful, hospitable, kind, and servant-hearted.

Without saying a word, the man watched her closely to learn whether or not the LORD had made his journey successful. When the camels had finished drinking, the man took out a gold nose ring weighing a beka and two gold bracelets weighing ten shekels. Then he asked, "Whose daughter are you? Please tell me, is there room in your father's house for us to spend the night?" She answered him, "I am the daughter of Bethuel, the son that Milkah bore to Nahor." And she added, "We have plenty of straw and fodder, as well as room for you to spend the night." Then the man bowed down and worshiped the LORD, saying, "Praise be to the LORD, the God of my master Abraham, who has not abandoned his kindness and faithfulness to my master. As for me, the LORD has led me on the journey to the house of my master's relatives." (Genesis 24:21–27)

Rebekah displayed respect, generosity, and a willingness to serve. After the servant told her family how he was seeking a wife for Abraham's son and all that transpired, they realized, *"This is from the LORD"* (Genesis 24:50). The servant gave Rebekah and her family many costly gifts; she willingly agreed to marry Isaac and left with Eliezer the very next day. Interestingly, her family blessed her like God had blessed Abraham, saying:

Our sister, may you increase to thousands upon thousands; may your
offspring possess the cities of their enemies. (Genesis 24:60)

At the end of their journey, the travelers came upon Isaac, who was meditating on God in a field. Need I say more? Anyone, man or woman, should seek God and the Holy Spirit will answer. God brought Isaac and Rebekah together. He is still in the matchmaking business. Marriage doesn't define you, but it can bless you if you do life and marriage with His leading.

WHAT ABOUT FINANCES?

Notice that in this story, Abraham's servant gave Rebekah some gold jewelry at the well and later presented many gifts both to her and her family. It's still appropriate for men to financially prepare for a wife and work diligently to provide for her before marriage. The servant said, *"The Lord has blessed my master abundantly, and he has become wealthy"* (Genesis 24:35). He made it clear at the onset that Isaac had the means to provide for Rebekah *thanks to God.*

IT'S STILL APPROPRIATE FOR MEN TO FINANCIALLY PREPARE FOR A WIFE AND WORK DILIGENTLY TO PROVIDE FOR HER BEFORE MARRIAGE.

As a financial expert, Gary has seen the finances of thousands of singles and married couples. Whether you're a man or a woman, being single is not a license to spend frivolously with no thought of the Lord or your future. Often, single persons are in a worse financial situation than married couples, even though their income may be greater and dependents fewer. I'm not sure what accounts for this. Perhaps it's a pervasive cultural attitude that being single is the time to be selfish… an *eat, drink, and be merry* adolescence that extends into adulthood… the feeling of independence… or a lack of self-control, or another voice of accountability.

Singleness doesn't mean we are not accountable to God for our financial decisions. If you hope to be married *someday*, treat your finances as if you were married *now*. Be wise and stay out of debt. Start early and save instead of spend. Submit this area to God to help qualify yourself as a wise woman or trustworthy man. Organize your finances or get help to do so and live a self-disciplined life led by the Holy Spirit. Don't put it off.

Regardless of whether you are married, will marry, or will remain single, all of us will experience a wedding day when Jesus returns. Christ will come to us, the church, as a bridegroom comes to his bride. There will be a wedding feast and every tear of sorrow will be wiped away. Single or married, happily serve Him with your whole heart until that day.

13

A NEW LIFESTYLE FOR HOME AND BUSINESS

Sheets of rain poured down as I whipped into the parking lot of my favorite *brands for less* store. I scurried with three children in tow to the formal dress area. I had to quickly locate the right outfit for our vendor's annual convention. Gary was going to receive the top award for the number one office in the nation. We had both worked hard and, remarkably, this honor came while pastoring a new church.

In our local office, I had worked many late nights to design and market a contest to motivate our sales team. Each month, I would take the children to a copy store to print the newsletter. Sometimes, I would give them a job as well. I typically scheduled the award's meetings, lined up hotels, and did promotions, creating slogans, décor, and awards. I took my turn speaking at meetings and during the week, I did underwriting and handled various other duties, including cleaning the office restrooms to save janitorial fees.

Gary was a faithful, steady salesperson, more of an educator who genuinely cared about people's financial success and worked steadily when others made excuses. I was the fiery passion, the why—for faith and family was my heart's cry. When speaking, I would paint the picture of freedom from a nine-to-five job, where vacations were minimal and family life was dismal as others educated their children. Gary and I desperately wanted families free from debt. It was in our hearts to help them live life abundantly instead of selling themselves like slaves. We had tasted freedom and passionately wanted it for everyone! It's what motivated us to work hard and make many sacrifices.

It had been a busy year, but now our hard work was paying off in a huge way. Our earnings had begun to soar; finally, after many years of struggle and penny-pinching, we were seeing God's promotion in our business. Ever since we had decided to pastor a small group of about forty people, our business was also aligning with God's Word. *"Seek first the kingdom of God and his righteousness, and all these things will be added to you"* (Matthew 6:33 ESV) was becoming a reality. Plans to build a house on our own acreage and take some amazing vacations with our children were finally coming to pass. These were far-reaching dreams after nine years of renting and living in a nineteenth century farmhouse and going to state park hotels for vacation!

So there I was in the store, managing my cart through crowded aisles with our five-year-old jumping off and on the end. I spotted a dressy satin double-breasted silver pantsuit with large rhinestone buttons. Perfect! I had learned to spy out deals on great clothes, always enjoying fashion but not having the finances to buy at upscale stores. I had also learned to do my makeup, start to finish, in five minutes flat. What else can a mother do when she wants to look good? I never thought motherhood was an excuse to let myself go and I saw it as part of honoring my husband and God. (I admit I had plenty of tracksuit days, too!)

Three days later, Gary and I arrived in Vancouver and checked into the sleek convention hotel. But the glam was overshadowed by the city. I was shocked to see such poverty. There were young people openly sleeping on the city streets or sharing a joint. For this naive mama who was doing everything I could to protect my family, it was beyond disturbing.

I was also troubled to see that many of the representatives attending the convention did so without their wives. Let's just say that it was *not* a family-friendly atmosphere. Alcohol flowed freely and I had to repeatedly say, "No, thank you!" I felt completely out of place as the award ceremony began. Then I spotted the wife of one of our sales team members… wearing a pantsuit identical to mine, except in red. I had to laugh! What else can you do? We looked like blonde twins. I was just glad I opted for the silver instead of the red.

As the moment came for my husband to take the stage, they shared his outstanding achievements for the year. There were cheers as they called his name. Gary quickly grabbed my hand and pulled me to my feet. Now I was in tow as we took the stage *together*! In accepting the award, Gary said, "I could not have done it without her."

Several people surrounded us after the event. A couple corporate leaders said they really appreciated the fact that Gary had his wife join him to receive the award. And in the following years' convention awards ceremonies, spouses were called up to the stage with the sales representatives. Their names were even included on the awards! I had not pushed for this, but Gary modeled it. God and my husband honored my effort as a co-laborer in a bigger mission, to demonstrate His kingdom and marriage. I had leaned on God, gave my best, and He promoted us together.

GOD AND MY HUSBAND HONORED MY EFFORT AS A CO-LABORER IN A BIGGER
MISSION, TO DEMONSTRATE HIS KINGDOM AND MARRIAGE.

That model began a ministry opportunity for us. Through many years, we were able to minister and pray for couples at conventions and in our business. The company we were part of transformed into a more family-friendly, marriage-honoring place. Every year, we saw more Christians join the ranks and met many lovely couples who sometimes brought their children along, encouraging one another in the faith. I like to think we had some impact on the attitudes that made these changes.

Locally, some of our business clients and representatives began to attend our newer church and it grew. Eventually, we started broadcasting and were suddenly thrust into a weekly radio program on marriage. Apparently, the couple who previously hosted the show got into a heated argument on-air. The station contacted us and in one week, we were their replacements. Every week, we struggled to feel adequate to teach other married couples—*live* on the radio! Fear would grip us as we drove to the station each Tuesday night, but we received many calls from listeners and prayed with couples, sometimes for an hour or more. After the show, we had a late dinner together. That was our date night! The sober reminder of couples whose marriages were in trouble kept us working through any challenges our own marriage encountered.

Eventually, this gave way to us beginning to share Gary's biblical teachings about finances and the kingdom of God on television. By the Holy Spirit's strong unction, I was actually the catalyst that pushed him into this arena. Once again, Gary asked me to join him by his side. I think he wanted me along since we had no clue what to do, but we usually managed to model the biblical truth, *"Two are better than one"* (Ecclesiastes 4:9). We didn't necessarily know *how* to do these things, but together, we learned and worked hard toward the mission. Our children joined us, creating an opening and jingle for our Faith Life Now program. Our daughter Amy shared the few resources we created in on-air spots. As God opened the door, we joined together to utilize our strengths to accomplish the seemingly impossible: a family, a business, and a ministry!

I LIKE TO THINK OF MARRIAGE AS A THREE-LEGGED RACE.
WE CAN EITHER LEARN TO WORK IN SYNC AND HARMONY, OR WE CAN FIGHT EACH
OTHER, SO THAT BOTH OF US LOSE THE RACE.

WE'RE IN THIS TOGETHER

I like to think of marriage as a three-legged race. Our legs are tied together. We are one (see Genesis 2:24) and we can either learn to work in sync and harmony, or we can fight each other, so that both of us lose the race, which also means our children's defeat. I see couples who kick or trip their partner as they attempt to run down the lane as if they weren't connected, and when they fall down, they blame their spouse. The Bible says a wife *"is the glory of man"* (1 Corinthians 11:7). What is glory but the presence and magnificence of God… shiny silver pantsuit and all!

The plan that unfolded in our lives—to share our faith through our profession, develop a business together as husband and wife, and eventually to pastor—is also illustrated in the relationship of Priscilla and Aquila, who are mentioned six times in the New Testament, always together. We know they traveled with the apostle Paul. The three were all tentmakers, connecting on a professional level and in ministry.

> *Paul left Athens and went to Corinth. There he met a Jew named Aquila, a native of Pontus, who had recently come from Italy with his wife Priscilla, because Claudius had ordered all Jews to leave Rome. Paul went to see them, and because he was a tentmaker as they were, he stayed and worked with them.* (Acts 18:1–3)

Paul speaks of this couple *together* every time he mentions them. He had an obvious gratitude for their devotion to God, to him, and to the early church. In his letter to the Romans, he says:

> *Greet Priscilla and Aquila, my co-workers in Christ Jesus. They risked their lives for me. Not only I but all the churches of the Gentiles are grateful to them.* (Romans 16:3)

We know that this couple's role was significant because they oversaw a home church and community in Ephesus and mentored Apollos as a minister. *"When Priscilla and Aquila heard [Apollos], they invited him to their home and explained to him the way of God more adequately"* (Acts 18:26). Apparently, Apollos needed more instruction on Jesus's teachings and God entrusted him to this husband-wife team.

Christian church buildings were not erected until the third century, so the couple hosted the church in Ephesus. We know that Priscilla became a spiritual mother and leader in her community. In one of his letters, Paul writes, *"Aquila and Prisca [Priscilla's nickname], together with the church in their house, send you hearty greetings in the Lord"* (1 Corinthians 16:19 ESV). *Together*—what a beautiful word that describes how Priscilla and Aquila worked. They were partners in business, ministry, and life as lovers and soul mates!

In four of the mentions of this power couple, Priscilla is listed first. Some biblical scholars say her leadership contribution may have been more significant than Aquila's, but it's just as likely an honor given to a woman who became the mainstay in the community. Their togetherness wasn't one of who came first because they put Jesus first. Paul would not have mentioned Priscilla unless he considered her contribution to the church at least as significant as her husband's.

This power couple had the ability to navigate a business together. They also uprooted and established a home multiple times not only for themselves but also for the believers of their community. What if every Christian couple, as business owners, worked together and did ministry of some sort? In over twenty-five years of ministry, we have celebrated and encouraged couples who have chosen this path. It's not easy to merge two wills, differing ideas, and gifts together. Yet isn't that what marriage is? Those who do the hard work will reap the rewards of their labor.

IT'S NOT EASY TO MERGE TWO WILLS, DIFFERING IDEAS, AND GIFTS TOGETHER, BUT THAT'S WHAT MARRIAGE IS.

With this in mind, I'd like to share a few stories of some modern power couples who are proving that women and men succeed when they work together.

MODERN POWER TEAMS

BERT AND STEPHANIE

Bert and Stephanie have overcome incredible obstacles together in marriage, family, business, and health. While raising children and building a demanding business, there were many moments of pressure and discouragement, but they committed to putting God first in their business and raising a champion family that serves the Lord.

Working behind the scenes with the children, Stephanie prayed for her family and Bert, becoming a source of encouragement to keep their eyes on the Lord when the pressures seemed insurmountable. Bert's tremendous acumen for business brought success, and the blessing of the Lord enriched them as they both, in agreement, sought to help fund His assignments. They stayed faithful to their word—they put God first in their marriage and business and learned to thrive as a team. As their business prospered,

Bert shared his financial learnings about the kingdom of God with others. Their success multiplied, and their business rose to number one and number three in the nation against businesses in their industry in much stronger markets—a seemingly impossible feat!

The enemy attempted to stop their influence. Bert had a brush with death as he was hemorrhaging from a procedure in the hospital. When his blood pressure dropped to 50/30 and the trauma team surrounded Bert, Stephanie went to war for his life. She declared Bert would "live and not die, and declare the works of the Lord." (See Psalm 118:17.) Bert's bleeding stopped miraculously, preventing him from a life-altering emergency surgery. Stephanie's tenacity to emerge from behind the scenes and fight the good fight of faith brought Bert through and increased their impact even more.

Bert and Stephanie share the importance of living from the Spirit and not allowing soulish struggles in marriage to stop their assignment and success. After forty-seven years of marriage, they have built a champion family, raising three successful children and nine grandchildren. They are having kingdom impact as a team, much like Priscilla and Aquila, and God has blessed their business and family.

KARA AND JUDD

Kara and Judd had just begun to build both a family of young children and their business when he was diagnosed with stage four cancer and given four days to live. Applying Gary's Bible teachings about healing, they sought God with everything in them, praying earnestly about treatments they should pursue and receiving prayer by the laying on of hands. (See, for example, Mark 16:18; Luke 4:40; Acts 28:8.)

Judd recovered! And now, he and Kara share their faith and his story with others, inviting them to church and mentoring them in business. They see their business and church as complementary forces to advance the kingdom of God.

STEVE AND MINDY

Steve and Mindy had worked together in the construction/building industry, but after an economic downturn, they saw little to no hope of reversing their financial failure. Things got so bad that at one point, they fought about who would commit suicide, thinking the surviving spouse and children would be better off without them. That's when someone invited them to our ministry.

At first, they thought the messages they heard were too good to be true, but their children loved the church, so they kept returning. Eventually, they decided to enter into business again, this time to build the kingdom of God by helping people get out of the stranglehold of debt. In gratitude to God who saved them, they continue to work side-by-side, traveling across the nation, helping to coordinate biblical financial seminars, and overseeing business management.

"We've never worked harder, but we love what we do!" says Mindy. Along the way, they enjoy dining at top restaurants, Steve's favorite pastime, and visiting new places, which Mindy loves. "If you are willing and obedient, you will eat the best of the land," she says.

KEITH AND KATHY

Keith and Kathy were just beginning to understand how the kingdom of God can operate on earth when Keith lost his job. They weren't sure how to proceed, but they decided to trust the Lord.

Keith started his own trucking company with just him and God's provision for a truck. He and Kathy kept trusting God, giving money to His works and praying He would bless theirs—and He did! Keith's business kept growing until they had a six-figure income. They were making more monthly than he used to make in a year.

Today, their income has quadrupled. They are a business team, but they also have become a strong ministry team, sharing the kingdom wherever they can.

BUILDING A POWER TEAM

Families working together in the same business is a historical model that was common well into the mid-twentieth century. Typically, a father would mentor his son in a business that would eventually become his. A husband and wife would work as a team and involve their children. In this way, the family was able to remain close and pass along their values and culture to the next generation.

Sadly, small businesses have been swallowed by large corporations and most people today work like indentured slaves, with long hours and short vacations. At the same time, public educational institutions indoctrinate children in beliefs that are in opposition to their parents'.

Thankfully, with home-based businesses, Internet capabilities, and home education, many couples are reestablishing the family business model. Some mothers leave outside jobs to become mompreneurs. Working together to establish a business has challenges, but a couple's relational foundations will have as much to do with their success as the business itself.

WORKING TOGETHER TO ESTABLISH A BUSINESS HAS CHALLENGES, BUT A COUPLE'S RELATIONAL FOUNDATIONS WILL HAVE AS MUCH TO DO WITH THEIR SUCCESS AS THE BUSINESS ITSELF.

So, how does this work?

As in every successful business, there must be a leader who bears the final responsibility for the organization. God placed the man as the chief executive officer (CEO) in the marriage, the head of the family, while his wife often functions as a chief operating officer (COO), responsible for the day-to-day operations. He ultimately must give an account to God for his family's overall well-being. This is a daunting task that can be intimidating and heavy since most men have not been trained how to lead and very few have seen it modeled well. Leadership can look glamorous, but those in charge feel the weight of responsibility because it requires laying down your life for those you lead.

As any great leader recognizes, success emanates from surrounding yourself with other leaders who understand and have experience in areas in which you are not as knowledgeable. Although a husband gives a direct account for the family's success, he needs the input, gifts, and perspective of his wife. She has wisdom and, as we discussed, different wiring and the ability to see things he doesn't always see, especially in the midst of pressure. A wise CEO will listen to the COO and team—sons, daughters, or staff—and utilize their strengths. They will also share the reward and accomplishments.

SUCCESS EMANATES FROM SURROUNDING YOURSELF WITH
OTHER LEADERS WHO UNDERSTAND AND HAVE EXPERIENCE IN AREAS IN
WHICH YOU ARE NOT AS KNOWLEDGEABLE.

IDENTIFYING STRENGTHS AND WEAKNESSES

A husband and wife bring differing abilities and strengths into a marriage and business. It would be very advantageous to take an inventory of each person's strengths and potential areas of vulnerability to weakness. This will enable you to assign differing tasks to the person with the strongest gifting and balance the responsibilities so that one person is not overly taxed or unable to focus on the highest priority for the team.

These are simple principles and practices that cause success in any endeavor. What are the couple's goals? Which items are negotiables and which are not? If training children and building a business are the couple's highest goals, how will they accomplish this and who will be responsible for what assignments? Even though they will ultimately do it together, each will have different responsibilities.

OUR FOUNDATION

Gary and I knew a few of these that became the foundation for everything else. We established that:

ALLEGIANCE

God would come first in our marriage and life, meaning His Word would be the umpire or voice.

FAMILY

We would personally invest in our children and teach them God's Word.

BUSINESS AND MINISTRY

We would build a business to fund ministry, like Paul the tentmaker and minister, to give us the ability to do ministry without being manipulated by financial need.

These were three bedrock decisions we made that helped us define all of the other decisions we would make throughout the years.

DEVISING A STRATEGY

The next question is, how will you accomplish this? And who will do what? You need to come up with a strategy that will give you the day-to-day responsibilities to accomplish the overall goals. We decided day-to-day that Gary would be the primary business leader and I would oversee the children's training. Obviously, we both shared and pitched in with support in both areas, but we each took more responsibility for our area. Sometimes, it wasn't easy to stick to these commitments, but we are glad we did!

There was a time when our finances were tight and I heard repeatedly from other voices, "If you would just go to work full-time like other women, you wouldn't have to struggle." Each time I was tempted to do just that, God gave me a strong rebuke for considering a move in the wrong direction. God clearly directing us to stay on the path we were on. I was home with the children, but I helped with the business. Gary was pursuing the business, but supported me and our children as a father and gave me some needed breaks. Our roles in either endeavor were not less but different and neither of us would have succeeded without the other.

I am sometimes asked by women who have started a business how to navigate who is in charge, her or her husband? That is an issue to be decided between the husband and wife. As long as they're in agreement, either one can be the CEO. I ask who is the stronger business person? Who has time? What are the other priorities? How will it affect those? To everything, there is a season. It may be that before children or at certain ages, it's easier for one person to oversee larger decisions and the other to manage, or vice versa. Or that only one person handles it entirely, but hires help for areas that are task-oriented.

The overall family leadership responsibility lies with the husband, but that doesn't mean that many operations can't lie under the wife's charge, giving her freedom and finances to direct those as she sees fit. Every marriage is unique; responsibilities must be calculated, weighed, and prayed. Ultimately, how can two walk together unless they are in agreement? Both husbands and wives must contribute to a plan that will bring the best results for their faith, family, and finances.

BOTH HUSBANDS AND WIVES MUST CONTRIBUTE TO A PLAN THAT WILL BRING THE BEST RESULTS FOR THEIR FAITH, FAMILY, AND FINANCES.

RAISING A FAMILY TOGETHER

People ask us how we raised five children who love and serve God. We loved Him and served Him and each other. All the rest was simply figuring out how to do that every day.

Writing his last letter as he faced death in Rome, Paul made sure to send final greetings to Priscilla and Aquila. (See 2 Timothy 4:19.) The couple had not only worked together loyally in both business and ministry, but they also demonstrated that same loyalty during their sixteen-year friendship with Paul—in hardships, in evangelism, and in opening their home, life, and business to Paul and the church. Loyalty to one another and to the mission became the landmark of their marriage and life. There is no greater testimony of learning to lean on.

If a man or woman cannot pass this test at home, then they can't be overseers in ministry. I personally have learned to look at how a woman talks about and treats her husband as a gauge for how she will treat any ministry assignment. Women who show contempt for their husband will also be disloyal in ministry if tested. The same holds true for men who are unwilling to share the credit for success with their wife. This is a spiritual maturity test that we have all failed at times, myself included.

When we do fail, we can get back up by saying, "I'm sorry." Make it right. Grow up in the Word of God together. Determine to keep working together. If we don't learn to follow, we cannot lead.

Marriage is the greatest place of immediate feedback on our spiritual growth and maturity. Working together just fast-tracks the process! If you can't love your brother or sister who you see, how can you say you love God? Your love and commitment will be tested in business or ministry, but ultimately, it will be tested anyway, so if you have the Holy Spirit's leading, don't be afraid to go for it.

14

IS THERE EVER A TIME TO BE NASTY?

At some point in your life, you will meet someone who is truly nasty. We know that Satan uses people to try to pervert God's principles and spread evil. Although we want to do everything in love, we also have to be wise to the schemes of the enemy. Jesus told his twelve apostles:

> I am sending you out like sheep among wolves. Therefore be as shrewd as snakes and as innocent as doves.   (Matthew 10:16)

So what do you do when somebody is blatantly standing for evil?

How do you handle a Jezebel spirit?

Is there ever a time when it's okay to be nasty?

Nastiness is never the answer, but there are times when we have to boldly call evil what it is and stand for righteousness. Jesus called out a select group of Pharisees for their words and thoughts, saying, *"You brood of vipers, how can you who are evil say anything good? For the mouth speaks what the heart is full of"* (Matthew 12:34).

Jesus was speaking to the blatant evil consuming their hearts and the spirits that were operating against God's plans for His people. Jesus did not tolerate lies or manipulation in the guise of religion. He brought true light whereas the enemy masqueraded as an angel of light through the Pharisees and religious teachers. Jesus spent time correcting inaccurate

166 NASTY GETS US NOWHERE

religious doctrines and situations that painted a false picture of God as a hard taskmaster. These Pharisees didn't have the heart of God toward the very people they were called to help. It wasn't an oversight. Their pride had aligned them with Satan's agenda.

In another instance, Jesus told the Pharisees, *"You belong to your father, the devil"* (John 8:44). This wasn't a nasty put-down. It was a confrontation with truth concerning their allegiance. They knew what they were choosing and He spoke directly to the fact that they were operating under the influence of the same spirit present in the garden of Eden, the serpent that is anti-Christ, anti-family, anti-marriage, and anti-people.

There are times we must do as Jesus did, calling out the maniacal plots of Satan through people. God uses strong women and strong men to stand up against evil. If we don't call out the plots of the enemy, evil will spread in our lives and laws.

> IF WE DON'T CALL OUT THE PLOTS OF THE ENEMY,
> EVIL WILL SPREAD IN OUR LIVES AND LAWS.

BIBLICAL WOMEN LEADERS

The religious world has often celebrated men who accomplish great things for God, but hasn't always known what to do with women achievers. The Bible celebrates women for their noble deeds and so should we. The Scriptures are replete with examples of strong women leaders who had hearts submitted to God.

Deborah saw the injustice and the disintegration of life in the land. (See Judges 4.) She saw the violence, the bondage, and the pains of oppression. Deeply troubled, she confronted a man named Barak who had the authority and power to act, but lacked the courage. Barak, reduced to fear and intimidation, asked Deborah to put her life on the line and go to battle with him against the forces of evil and Sisera, the commander of Canaan's army.

"Certainly I will go with you," said Deborah. "But because of the course you are taking, the honor will not be yours, for the LORD will deliver Sisera into the hands of a woman." So Deborah went with Barak to Kedesh. (Judges 4:9)

Deborah was described as a prophetess, a mother to the nation; that day, God used her passion and discernment to bring about the destruction of Sisera and his army. Her conviction and confrontation saved Israel, God's nation. And as Deborah prophesied, a woman killed Sisera, driving a tent peg through his head while he slept. (See Judges 4:21.) That's nasty business, but it was God's business to free his people. God will use men or women in many ways to bring about His plans.

Queen Esther risked her life for her cousin Mordecai and her people, the Jews. When Haman sought to destroy them, he was killed instead. (See the book of Esther.) The Samaritan woman who met Jesus at the well gave up her past life of sin and evangelized her town. (See John 4:7–42.) When David was living in the wilderness with his troops and needed provisions, Abigail stepped in to feed them. (See 1 Samuel 25.) Women supported Jesus's ministry against the enemy's lies so He could bring healing and salvation everywhere He went. And the list goes on! Like the many male heroes in the Bible, these women were used mightily by God. If we could simply work together in the kingdom, we too could see success. The world would stand up and take notice.

But the enemy keeps drawing Christians to radical ideologies. Christian Feminism Today, a website of the Evangelical and Ecumenical Women's Caucus, wants "metaphors for God to include biblical female imagery." One recent article suggests that the prophet Miriam wrote most of Genesis.[30] Another group, the Christian Feminist Network, which calls itself "LGBTQI-inclusive," has an article about "the fallacy of male strength."[31]

---

30. Rabbi Allen S. Maller, "Did Miriam the Prophet Write Down Most of Genesis and the First Part of Exodus?," March 12, 2020, Christian Feminism Today (eewc.com/did-miriam-the-prophet-write-down-most-of-genesis-and-the-first-part-of-exodus).
31. Robin Bunce, "Complementarity: the fallacy of male strength," November 2, 2019 (christianfeministnetwork.com/2019/01/08/complementarity-the-fallacy-of-male-strength).

In 2010, an article in *The Atlantic* magazine proclaimed, "We no longer need men" and "women will control everything."[32]

A few years later, *The Atlantic* ran an article highlighting Katelyn Beaty's book *A Woman's Place: A Christian Vision for Your Calling in the Office, the Home, and the World*. Beaty said she wanted to tell "wives and mothers that there is so much inherent goodness in the call to work and… we needn't pit certain types of roles against each other."[33] She went on to say:

> When you talk about scales of influence or scales of societal influence, a woman who is staying at home with [her] children isn't going to have as much influence on the direction of culture.… We can talk about motherhood as a specific type of calling, but I'm not ready to professionalize it.[34]

And yet motherhood can be one of the most impactful vocations a woman can experience.

Why do we put women in a position to fight over career *or* motherhood and thus devalue both options, which can occur at differing seasons or at the same time? This faulty reasoning of the feminist agenda is destructive to both faith and family.

Many years ago, my Bible studies took me to Isaiah 3 and 4. These chapters present a picture of judgment and a lack of leadership because much of Israel had turned from God and His Word. The youth had been led astray by a spirit of confusion from the women.

> *Youths oppress my people, women rule over them. My people, your guides lead you astray; they turn you from the path.* (Isaiah 3:12)

Women are so influential and important to the divine plan of God that when they turn away from His design, it results in confusion, especially for children. These youths were being mentored in a wrong direction by the very women who were called by God to nurture and care for them.

32. Hanna Rosin, "The End of Men," *The Atlantic*, July/August 2010 (www.theatlantic.com/magazine/archive/2010/07/the-end-of-men/308135).
33. Jonathan Merritt, "The Conservative, Christian Case for Working Women," *The Atlantic*, July 5, 2016 (www.theatlantic.com/politics/archive/2016/07/the-conservative-christian-case-for-working-women/490025).
34. Ibid.

As we read further, we get a clearer picture of the hearts and attitudes that these women possessed. Flirtatious and self-ambitious, they no longer honored the covenant of marriage. Does that sound familiar? Their disregard for the things of God and lust for self-indulgence left them without hair, a symbol of glory and headship. Their husbands, their providers and protectors, died by the sword, a judgment against their rebellion.

WOMEN ARE SO INFLUENTIAL AND IMPORTANT TO THE DIVINE PLAN OF GOD THAT WHEN THEY TURN AWAY FROM HIS DESIGN, IT RESULTS IN CONFUSION, ESPECIALLY FOR CHILDREN.

The LORD says, "The women of Zion are haughty, walking along with outstretched necks, flirting with their eyes, strutting along with swaying hips, with ornaments jingling on their ankles. Therefore the Lord will bring sores on the heads of the women of Zion; the LORD will make their scalps bald." In that day the Lord will snatch away their finery: the bangles and headbands and crescent necklaces, the earrings and bracelets and veils, the headdresses and anklets and sashes, the perfume bottles and charms, the signet rings and nose rings, the fine robes and the capes and cloaks, the purses and mirrors, and the linen garments and tiaras and shawls. Instead of fragrance there will be a stench; instead of a sash, a rope; instead of well-dressed hair, baldness; instead of fine clothing, sackcloth; instead of beauty, branding. Your men will fall by the sword, your warriors in battle. The gates of Zion will lament and mourn; destitute, she will sit on the ground. (Isaiah 3:16–26)

These women exchanged the beauty of marriage and family for the judgment of oppression, destruction, and lack. In the end, seven women fight over one man and beg to be called his wives.

In that day seven women will take hold of one man and say, "We will eat our own food and provide our own clothes; only let us be called by your name. Take away our disgrace!" (Isaiah 4:1)

This judgment of Israel parallels America and many other nations today. The stage is set and the same issues exist in our culture. I have watched in dismay as Christian women shun marriage, family, and even heterosexuality in the name of the Lord.

Following this dismal picture in Isaiah, God tells us that while His judgment is great, so is His answer.

> *In that day the Branch of the LORD will be beautiful and glorious, and the fruit of the land will be the pride and glory of the survivors.*
>
> (Isaiah 4:2)

In the midst of the rebellion that brings brokenness and judgment, God gives us His Son Jesus to provide the answer. Only He is able to heal the divide.

> *The Lord will wash away the filth of the women of Zion; he will cleanse the bloodstains from Jerusalem by a spirit of judgment and a spirit of fire. Then the LORD will create over all of Mount Zion and over those who assemble there a cloud of smoke by day and a glow of flaming fire by night; over everything the glory will be a canopy. It will be a shelter and shade from the heat of the day, and a refuge and hiding place from the storm and rain.*
>
> (Isaiah 4:4–6)

God is our refuge, our shelter, and our healing from the impact of the enemy's branding of sin, which stole our beautiful inheritance. It is now restored in Christ.

THE JEZEBEL SPIRIT

I had personally planned to stay as far as possible from even mentioning Jezebel in this book, but after encountering this spirit recently, I felt compelled by the Holy Spirit to address this issue. So what is a Jezebel spirit? Who qualifies? And how do you deal with it?

Too often, we've heard the murmurings of a woman being *a Jezebel* simply because she is a leader or has strong convictions to impact the kingdom of God. That's a divisive plot of evil in itself. Isn't that just like the enemy?

Jezebel instituted Baal worship in Israel and had the Lord's prophets killed. (See 1 Kings 16:31; 18:13.) Religious circles have used the phrase,

"She's a Jezebel" for years to identify everything from women who wore makeup to strong women who tried to step into leadership territory for God's kingdom. The biblical Jezebel is the epitome of nasty. Unfortunately, her mode of operation was not new on the scene, nor is it uniquely female.

Is a strong woman a *Jezebel* because she has a voice or convictions to create change? Not if her cause is righteous, her influence appropriate, and her alignment with proper authority. The same goes for men.

THE ORIGINAL JEZEBEL DEFIED GOD, ATTACKED AND KILLED HIS PROPHETS, AND BLASPHEMED HIS WORD.

The original Jezebel manipulated her husband out of self-ambition for gain. With a rebellious heart, she defied God, attacked and killed His prophets, and blasphemed His Word. She was responsible for encouraging idol worship and the killing of babies offered as sacrifices to false gods. Her motives were purely selfish and demon-crafted; she literally carried out the plans of hell against God's people, including women and children.

Many other examples of treachery like Jezebel's exist in Scripture, starting with the original act of Lucifer's rebellion in heaven repeated in the garden. The term *Jezebel spirit* was given to an evil, demon-inspired spirit that overtakes a person or movement to undermine God-given authority with the intent to divide and destroy. When Jesus called the Pharisees *a brood of vipers*, He was identifying this very spirit. The Pharisees didn't honor God with their hearts, only with their lips. They used religious language, but their hearts were not in alignment with God, thus they attacked Christ.

I prefer to refer to this spiritual operation as *anti-Christ* because it didn't start with a woman named Jezebel; it started with Satan leading a third of God's angels down a path of demonization. They were kicked out of heaven and have used the same operation against men and women throughout the ages. Many people have fallen victim to it, thwarting businesses, dividing ministries, and wrecking homes and nations.

The Jezebel spirit operates covertly, hiding behind flattery, and will try to get close to influencers or leaders until it gains enough power and sway to subvert them. Overcome with self-ambition, it will flatter to gain authority so it can one day take over. This is exactly how Satan operated in the garden. He was able to manipulate what God said to deceive Eve into doubting God's leadership. Then he moved in to take Adam and Eve's dominion over the earth. Satan, or the Jezebel spirit, envied the authority God had given them; lusting after their headship, he devised a plan to steal it.

THE JEZEBEL SPIRIT OPERATES COVERTLY, HIDING BEHIND FLATTERY, AND WILL TRY TO GET CLOSE TO INFLUENCERS OR LEADERS UNTIL IT GAINS ENOUGH POWER AND SWAY TO SUBVERT THEM.

Eve was infected with self-ambition (flattery) through false accusations about God (subversion of the true leader) and given a promise of independence (power). Knowledge is attractive and it feeds our self-ambition and pride. The enemy promises to give us the world's power if we will just bow down and worship him. But he's a proven liar and his promises end in embarrassment and destruction. He simply uses people as pawns until he's done with them. Then their life ends just like Jezebel's. Destroyed, dishonored, and alone, they face judgment. Nasty makes us lonely… and gets us nowhere. Jezebel's own servants threw her out a window, where she was trampled by horses and eaten by dogs. (See 2 Kings 9:32–37.)

The Jezebel spirit creates a tangled web of deceit that lays a trap for leaders and followers. It makes leaders want to quit and those under their protection seek to rebel. Why have men stopped leading and protecting? They quit! Many women rebelled against authority, and that has caused chaos and confusion in their lives as well.

The Jezebel spirit divides and creates disloyalty until homes, churches, businesses, and nations are so divided that destruction soon follows. Satan comes to steal, kill, and destroy. (See John 10:10.) He steals respect, kills authority, and destroys both leader and follower if he can. Without leadership, we are lost indeed. Who mentors the next generation of young men or young women? Men have abandoned family. Women are demanding their own ambitions over family. Lost without love or leadership, children commit suicide.

THIS JEZEBEL SPIRIT IS NOT FEMALE OR MALE. WOMEN ARE NOT THE ONLY ONES SUSCEPTIBLE TO THIS DEMON-INSPIRED MANEUVER OF THE ENEMY.

This Jezebel spirit is not female or male. Women are not the only ones susceptible to this demon-inspired maneuver of the enemy in the home, church, or business.

I knew a talented female worship leader who had a male assistant. Both were under the authority of the pastor, who had appointed them. The male assistant worked against the worship leader, subverted her authority, and attempted to steal her position. He tried to get her removed by using deceptive maneuvers and making sure to covertly expose her faults to others. He flattered coworkers while tarnishing her. This is typical of the Jezebel spirit.

The assistant's goal was to create division among the leader's team, so that when things collapsed, he could replace her. His self-ambition resulted in disloyalty.

God's Word encourages us:

Do nothing out of selfish ambition or vain conceit. Rather, in humility value others above yourselves, not looking to your own interests but each of you to the interests of the others. (Philippians 2:3–4)

Ambition to accomplish a goal can be a great asset, but without submission to the proper authority, it creates chaos, confusion, and division.

We can probably agree that there is room for a change in how women and men work together to breach the divide between us. To get nasty with each other only puts us in the enemy's camp, separating us from God, just as it did in the garden. It's a different era, but the same operation.

Instead of the body of Christ learning to work together as men and women, we keep fighting and falling for divisive, nasty, self-serving attitudes. Why are we allowing the world's system, dominated by self-ambition and dissension, to infiltrate our faith camp to discredit the gospel and pit us against one another? Nasty rebellion hasn't gotten the world anywhere—and it won't get the faith community any further.

**NASTY REBELLION HASN'T GOTTEN THE WORLD ANYWHERE—
AND IT WON'T GET THE FAITH COMMUNITY ANY FURTHER.**

We live in a time of great treachery and deceit, with people loving themselves more than they love God, placing greater value on themselves than they do His ways. It's time to truthfully confront evil; at the same time, we need to show mercy to those caught in sinful behavior. To survive, the pendulum must swing back to truth and the values of respect, loyalty, honor, kindness, and teamwork. We can make that happen through prayer and personal change.

Stand up to evil and pray for those caught in its hold. And when lives depend on it, make war on evil.

Choose life, so that you and your children may live and that you may love the LORD your God, listen to his voice, and hold fast to him.
(Deuteronomy 30:19–20)

15

SUCCEEDING TOGETHER IN HARD TIMES

A furious storm came suddenly on the Sea of Galilee, where the disciples had fished for most of their lives. Frightened, they awakened Jesus, saying, *"Teacher, don't you care if we drown?"* (Mark 4:38). They drew the conclusion that they were going to die and, in the same breath, accused Jesus of not caring! Have you ever been frustrated with life and said, "God, don't you care?"

Cleaning house, I spotted my daughter Amy's open diary on her bed. I knew I shouldn't, but I couldn't resist the urge to pick it up. I read her latest entry, left in plain sight. She shared her loneliness, her desire to have a husband, and her belief that God would provide one. At the same time, she was also battling a tumor in her abdomen. It had been growing for several years and it made her look pregnant. As I read her diary, I felt her heart's yearning and hurt for her as a parent.

I thought, *Why isn't she healed by now?* If anyone deserved healing, it was Amy. I knew her devotion and it hurt to read her words of pain and sorrow. In a moment of emotion and doubt, I said to God, "She's been so faithful to you! Don't you care?!"

Sometimes, people say or do things in pressure-filled moments that are regrettable; circumstances can drown our faith in sorrow. That's why we have to give each other a lot of grace. My words revealed my own lack of faith and understanding of how God's kingdom works.

God quickly reminded me that He gave Amy to me—and He loves her even more than I do!

I quickly fell to my knees crying and repented to God for thinking and voicing such doubt. I renewed my belief in Him, "Lord, I do believe You!" I knew He was the answer and always fulfills His promises. When we feel afraid and are not leaning on Him in trust, we can think and draw the wrong conclusions just like the disciples did in the storm. It wasn't God who did this to my daughter. He was not to blame. Satan steals, kills, and destroys, and then blames it on God.

SATAN STEALS, KILLS, AND DESTROYS, AND THEN BLAMES IT ON GOD.

In a short while, God sent a young man to work in our ministry. Jason Freudiger had been working at another ministry, where he had been crying out to God, just as Amy had, to direct his future and bring his marriage partner. Both in their late twenties, Amy and Jason started as friends, but it didn't take long for them to realize this was God's answer. A year later, they were married.

Both felt strongly that Amy must be healed before they could pursue having a family. Amy details the account in her book, *Healed Overnight*.[35] She became so convinced of God's plan to heal her that when she came to church for prayer, she declared it was already done. "I am healed," she said. Two weeks later, she woke to find the tumor had disappeared overnight, without surgery or any intervention. There was no explanation… except God. Today, Amy and Jason have three beautiful children.

At times of pressure, we all feel like fainting, quitting, or giving up, but we must become established and never stop trusting that God has given us precious promises that belong to us. God is not the problem—He's the answer! Amy later told me that she had hoped for God to heal her and prayed for healing, but it wasn't until she let the promises of Scripture drive out all doubt that it happened.

---

35. Amy Keesee Freudiger, *Healed Overnight: My Encounter With the Supernatural* (Honest Beauty Publishing, 2016).

Blessed is the one who does not walk in step with the wicked or stand in the way that sinners take or sit in the company of mockers, but whose delight is in the law of the Lord, *and who meditates on his law day and night. That person is like a tree planted by streams of water, which yields its fruit in season and whose leaf does not wither—**whatever they do prospers.*** (Psalm 1:1–3)

Learning to lean on God and becoming planted in His ways is a process that develops trust. Just like a tree, we must be rooted in God's Word, unmoved by society's storms. The enemy wants to uproot our faith before it can grow strong enough to produce good fruit. God is patient and kind with us in the journey to learn to lean on His understanding as well as develop our faith.

I believe all leaders who love Jesus share Paul's heart:

I want you to know how hard I am contending for you and for those at Laodicea, and for all who have not met me personally. My goal is that they may be encouraged in heart and united in love, so that they may have the full riches of complete understanding, in order that they may know the mystery of God, namely, Christ, in whom are hidden all the treasures of wisdom and knowledge. I tell you this so that no one may deceive you by fine-sounding arguments. For though I am absent from you in body, I am present with you in spirit and delight to see how disciplined you are and how firm your faith in Christ is. So then, just as you received Christ Jesus as Lord, continue to live your lives in him, rooted and built up in him, strengthened in the faith as you were taught, and overflowing with thankfulness. See to it that no one takes you captive through hollow and deceptive philosophy, which depends on human tradition and the elemental spiritual forces of this world rather than on Christ. For in Christ all the fullness of the Deity lives in bodily form, and in Christ you have been brought to fullness. He is the head over every power and authority. (Colossians 2:1–10)

Paul was concerned for the well-being of the believers in Colossae and Laodicea, encouraging them to continue in their faith and not be deceived by the world or religion. Just as he did back then, Satan is waging an all-out war in this hour, trying to steal the hearts of people away from God. He's using the same tactics described in Scripture. Religious leaders and political oppression sent Jesus to the cross. These same forces were manipulated by the enemy to attack Paul and the other apostles and prophets of old. They drummed up fake witnesses and accused him of blasphemy against religious practice and of being an enemy of the government.

Although carried out by men and women, these practices did not originate with flesh and blood but rather from the enemy and his control over people who have not committed themselves wholly to Christ.

> *We know that we are children of God, and that the whole world is* **under the control** *of the evil one.* (1 John 5:19)

We can't be naïve. Some people are planted like weeds among the wheat to deceive and destroy. They are blinded by Satan and will do his bidding if allowed.

> *The god of this age has blinded the minds of unbelievers, so that they cannot see the light of the gospel that displays the glory of Christ, who is the image of God.* (2 Corinthians 4:4)

If we follow the blind guides of the world and its so-called wisdom, we will end up with their statistics of suicide, divorce, financial ruin, and spiritual chaos.

THE SPIRIT OF DIVISION

Accusation is one of the strategies Satan uses in an effort to create division. Just as Adam tried to blame Eve for their failure, Satan is accusing us day and night about what the Bible says. A stream of accusatory thoughts try to bombard all of our minds. And if he can't get us to receive his condemnation, he'll try to get us to condemn others. Just as he tried to divide heaven, the enemy seeks to divide the house of God and divide families. Satan knows a house divided cannot stand but will fall. He knows he must first tie us up before he can rob us. (See Mark 3:27.) That's why unity in a marriage, business, ministry, or family, coupled with submission to the spiritual authority that God has sanctioned, is crucial to resist the enemy's attacks and win in life.

Satan wants to divide your heart, your family, and your sphere of influence. A spirit of division can open doors to him without God's covenant to protect us. It works to magnify our differences, to incite disgust or hatred between genders, ethnicities, leaders, and followers. Satan wants to stop God's increase in your life and he does so with divisiveness and unforgiveness. He wiggles a little seed of doubt into our minds and hearts to get us out of agreement with the Word of God, or out of agreement with our spouse and the body of Christ.

Don't be ignorant of Satan's schemes! You are in a battle, but Satan cannot control you outside of your will, without your cooperation and consent. You must first recognize that you *are* in a battle. Many people choose not to believe that—some even deny that Satan exists—but it's true. Your unwillingness to engage in battle with Satan doesn't mean that the battle isn't raging; it just means you may lose. Once you realize the battle is real, you can learn to recognize what's going on and take the proper action to fight and transform the situation.

ONCE YOU REALIZE THE BATTLE WITH SATAN IS REAL,
YOU CAN LEARN TO RECOGNIZE WHAT'S GOING ON AND TAKE THE PROPER ACTION
TO FIGHT AND TRANSFORM THE SITUATION.

Don't be ignorant of Satan's schemes. Be sober-minded and vigilant because the devil walks around like a roaring lion, looking for people to devour. (See 1 Peter 5:8.) Resist him with steadfast faith.

We can see Satan's scheme to discourage, divide, and uproot believers illustrated in the lives of Barnabas and Paul. You are created for special assignments just as they were! Appointed by the Holy Spirit for a special mission, Barnabas and Paul began to travel and preach the good news of the gospel. In the city of Paphos on the island of Cyprus, they met a Jewish sorcerer and false prophet named Bar-Jesus, who was an attendant of the governor, Sergius Paulus. (See Acts 13:6–7). Think of Wormtongue from J. R. R. Tolkien's *The Lord of the Rings* series, who controlled King Théoden through sorcery. The governor wanted to hear the Word of God, but Bar-Jesus (also called Elymas) urged him not to listen to Barnabas or Paul. I love the incredible scene that played out next:

> *Saul, who was also called Paul, filled with the Holy Spirit, looked straight at Elymas and said, "You are a child of the devil and an enemy of everything that is right! You are full of all kinds of deceit and trickery. Will you never stop perverting the right ways of the Lord? Now the hand of the Lord is against you. You are going to be blind for a time, not even able to see the light of the sun." Immediately mist and darkness came over him, and he groped about, seeking someone to lead him by the hand. When the proconsul saw what had happened, he believed, for he was amazed at the teaching about the Lord.* (Acts 13:9–12)

After this, the two sailed to Pisidian Antioch in Turkey, where nearly the whole city came out to hear them preach the word of God.

WHEN YOU ARE GAINING TERRITORY IN THE KINGDOM, SATAN SENDS OFFENSE AND DIVISION TO TRY TO DISCOURAGE YOU.

After many years in ministry and leadership, what happens next doesn't surprise me. Satan doubled down on his counterattack. When you are gaining territory in the kingdom, Satan sends offense and division to try to discourage you.

> *When the Jews saw the crowds, they were filled with jealousy. They began to contradict what Paul was saying and heaped abuse on him. Then Paul and Barnabas answered them boldly: "We had to speak the word of God to you first. Since you reject it and do not consider yourselves worthy of eternal life, we now turn to the Gentiles. For this is what the Lord has commanded us: 'I have made you a light for the Gentiles, that you may bring salvation to the ends of the earth.'" When the Gentiles heard this, they were glad and honored the word of the Lord; and all who were appointed for eternal life believed. The word of the Lord spread through the whole region. But the Jewish leaders incited the God-fearing women of high standing and the leading men of*

the city. They stirred up persecution against Paul and Barnabas, and expelled them from their region. So they shook the dust off their feet as a warning to them and went to Iconium. And the disciples were filled with joy and with the Holy Spirit. (Acts 13:45–52)

Paul and Barnabas could have spent all of their time dealing with the offenses of the Jews. They could have gotten discouraged. Instead, they kept their focus on their mission and continued to take territory for the kingdom of God. That's how *we* have to be when dealing with division, strife, and offense.

When someone gives you offense, it doesn't mean you have to take it. —Joyce Meyer

PASSING THE TEST

Disputes in the church can be difficult and discouraging. Even though the leaders in our lives can make mistakes—whether a husband, parent, employer, or pastor—God appointed them to help us grow. Most of the time, good leaders are at least *trying* to get it right. But it is clear that there are those who have not qualified themselves who will attempt to create division and confusion in God-ordained relationships, whether it's your marriage, ministry, or workplace.

Certain people *came down from Judea to Antioch and were teaching the believers: "Unless you are circumcised, according to the custom taught by Moses, you cannot be saved."* (Acts 15:1)

Beware of *certain people!*

In our twenty-five years of pastoring, we have seen divisive people come in and try to create chaos in the lives of others. Sometimes, they think their methods are noble because of immaturity; other times, they are intent on creating disunity. In either instance, Scripture warns about those who cause such divisions. It never goes well for them or the people they infect with conflicting opinions and interpretations. Paul even admonishes us to warn a divisive person to stop and have nothing to do with them if they continue. (See Titus 3:10; Romans 16:17)

For such people are not serving our Lord Christ, but their own appe-
tites. By smooth talk and flattery they deceive the minds of naive
people. (Romans 16:18)

Nothing is more discouraging to a leader or other believers than to have
to deal with the accusations of *certain people* while already walking through
other pressures. Those causing trouble for the church in Antioch were not
apostles or leaders; they lacked God-ordained authority. Unlike them, Paul
submitted himself to Peter and the church at Jerusalem. He went to them
to handle the issue and receive direction. God's call was on Paul through a
radical conversion—Jesus spoke to him after He had already ascended to
His Father—yet Paul submitted himself to the apostles' authority. Paul
and Barnabas worked together to handle the accusations and difficulties
brought by certain people, legalists, and some religious women through
wisdom and authority. But the same spirit of division that had attempted
to divide the church previously attacked their personal relationship.

Some time later Paul said to Barnabas, "Let us go back and visit the
believers in all the towns where we preached the word of the Lord and
see how they are doing." Barnabas wanted to take John, also called
Mark, with them, but Paul did not think it wise to take him.... They
had such a sharp disagreement that they parted company.
(Acts 15:36–39)

Paul and Barnabas had come through so many difficulties brought on
by issues and people outside of their control, but now their problems were
inward. Perhaps they were weary. Barnabas apparently did not submit
himself to Paul's leadership and they split up over their disagreement. They
apparently never preached together again, although Paul later mentions
that Barnabas is worthy of financial support (see 1 Corinthians 9:6) and
even comes around to Barnabas's cousin, John-Mark, calling him a fellow
worker (see Philemon 1:24).

Paul evangelized the entire region and wrote the most books in the
New Testament. So was it more important for Barnabas to get his own
way, or submit to Paul's decision to not take Mark? It seems like a petty
issue after the incredible battles they had already faced and won. Paul had
dealt with a sorcerer, slander, religious women, and more, yet Barnabas left

him. Even so, God made everything work out because instead of one group spreading the gospel, there were now two.

I share this example to show how demonic outside forces can attack relationships and pressure can eventually divide people if there are not clear lines regarding authority or leadership responsibility. But it's also important, in any relationship, not to lose sight of the big picture. How many relationships survive hardships and then dissolve over a minor issue?

HOW MANY RELATIONSHIPS SURVIVE HARDSHIPS AND THEN DISSOLVE OVER A MINOR ISSUE?

No doubt, Paul had a strong personality. He needed one. He was beaten many times and dragged out of town; political and religious leaders sought to stop him everywhere he went. Humility to serve with Paul would have advanced Barnabas as well, but he didn't see it that way.

Barnabas was not a bad person. We're told, *"He was a good man, full of the Holy Spirit and faith, and a great number of people were brought to the Lord"* (Acts 11:24). Our relationships, commitments, and marriages can be birthed in the Holy Spirit and when we are full of the Spirit, they work. Yet in difficult times when the pressure gets intense or there are personal misunderstandings, it's easy to let go of the bigger picture and go our own way instead of God's. It happens in marriages, businesses, and every endeavor that involves people.

Barnabas did not pass the test. He was apparently offended and went his way. This is how the enemy divides. It's easy to get weary. Barnabas probably felt like Paul didn't care about Mark, but Paul knew that troubles and persecution awaited him and he couldn't take the risk that the mission would fail because Mark decided to desert him again. (See Acts 13:13.)

What does wisdom dictate in a choice like this? Barnabas seemed to focus on the need and potential of his cousin, but Paul was focusing on the demands and potential of the larger cause of the gospel. Paul was more concerned about the mission than pleasing Barnabas or Mark.

*Am I now trying to win the approval of human beings, or of God?… If
I were still trying to please people, I would not be a servant of Christ.*
(Galatians 1:10)

In Barnabas's absence, God sent a young man named Timothy for
Paul's mission. Timothy had a Jewish mother and a Greek father who had
not allowed him to be circumcised. Paul wanted to take Timothy on his
mission, *"so he circumcised him because of the Jews who lived in that area"*
(Acts 16:3). Paul wanted to avoid offense among the Jews and Timothy
could have fought it, yet he followed Paul's wisdom. Timothy became
Paul's spiritual son, a pastor, and later a bishop. He succeeded because he
could follow and eventually lead.

Paul commends Timothy repeatedly in his letters. (See, for example,
1 Timothy 1; Philippians 2:22.)

LEANING ON LEADERSHIP

It's important for us to learn to trust God by leaning on leaders in our
lives. There is protection, safety, and security in having guidance and leadership. Remember, the word *submission* means "to come under the loving
protection of." We live in a time where everything that *can* be shaken *is*
being shaken. For our faith to stand, we must stay in submission to God,
His Word, and systems of authority. We cannot have authority of our own
or operate in authority if we cannot properly respect and submit to it.

FOR OUR FAITH TO STAND, WE MUST STAY IN SUBMISSION TO GOD,
HIS WORD, AND SYSTEMS OF AUTHORITY.

When Jesus said something that some of His followers had a hard time
understanding, they *"turned back and no longer followed him"* (John 6:66).
But the twelve apostles were disciplined and submitted to Jesus's authority.
When He asked if they wanted to leave as well, Peter said, *"Lord, to whom
shall we go? You have the words of eternal life. We have come to believe and to
know that you are the Holy One of God"* (John 6:68–69).

Nehemiah submitted to the authority of his king, who permitted him to rebuild the walls of Jerusalem. (See Nehemiah 2.) Nehemiah shared his vision with the Israelites and when they heard that God had blessed the work, they agreed to help. They submitted to Nehemiah's authority to undertake this massive building project and post guards to fight the enemies hell-bent on stopping it.

As prime minister during World War II, Winston Churchill fought the overwhelming voice of his own party, which demanded that he surrender Britain to Hitler. In the midst of this great opposition, Churchill developed a plan to call upon his own people to surrender their boats to rescue more than 336,000 British and Allied soldiers who were trapped on the beaches in Dunkirk, France.

Nehemiah's plan succeeded, and so did Churchill's, but not without a fight. God has a good end to any endeavor He has asked of you, but anything worth doing is often met with some opposition. Opposition is not the proof you've missed God, but almost always the guarantee you're on to something that hits His mark. Surrendering is not an option we can afford. Too much is at stake.

OPPOSITION IS NOT THE PROOF YOU'VE MISSED GOD BUT ALMOST ALWAYS THE GUARANTEE YOU'RE ON TO SOMETHING THAT HITS HIS MARK.

HOW TO EXERCISE AUTHORITY

We can easily fall into the offenses and lies of misunderstanding because of our differences as men and women. More than this, however, we are wrestling with dark, evil forces that are inspiring the division between us. These dark forces are out to wreck our relationships. We must know our authority in Christ to stop them and help us see more clearly the real source of conflict.

We can do this by speaking God's words, using our authority to overcome the enemy by the blood of Jesus. We are submitted to Him, seated with Him in heavenly places, and now we exercise by command. We use the name of Jesus as our head and Lord to drive out sorcery and divisive spirits. Then we must work together and recognize the real source of confusion, division, and slander, *"making the most of every opportunity, because the days are evil"* (Ephesians 5:16).

It would be easy to cave in to the lies of culture, but there is a reward waiting for us that's greater than its approval—the eternal *"crown of righteousness"* (2 Timothy 4:8).

Thanks to Jesus and His redeeming work for us on the cross, you have authority over the enemy in relationships and any area of life in which you battle darkness. We overcome by the *blood of the Lamb* and the *word* of our testimony.

> *For everyone who has been born of God overcomes the world. And this is the victory that has overcome the world—our faith.*
>
> (1 John 5:4 ESV)

Outside of your work, your family, and your church, you have a choice regarding the kind of people you listen to, spend time with, and befriend. Are they mockers? Divisive? What kind of fruit is in their life from choices they've made? God rewards those who diligently seek Him. Do the people in your life have the fruit that comes from following God?

THE DIVISION IN OUR NATION AND IN OUR HOMES IS NOT OVER POLITICS BUT MORALITY.

There is division in our nation and in our homes over morality. It may appear to be political, but it's really a decision of whether to embrace truth or lies. The truth tells us that abortion is sinful and wrong. Anyone who supports it is party to it. Denying your freedom of religion or free speech is also wrong, yet we see an ever-increasing pressure against voices of faith. Persecuting Christians or churches is wrong. Anyone who is party to it is persecuting the Lord Jesus Christ. We know this from Paul's experience on the road to Damascus. (See Acts 9:4.)

You, dear children, are from God and have overcome [evil spirits], because the one who is in you is greater than the one who is in the world. (1 John 4:4)

Make a commitment that you are not going to be led by cultural lies. Be determined to pass the test and not miss God and His blessing. Ask yourself, "Who can correct me?"

In the early days of my faith, my pastor sent me a letter asking that I return a late book to the church library. I was immature and quickly offended, thinking, "I gave my money to them!" The Holy Spirit dealt with my attitude. I had to think about my wrong action and recognize that I did not handle things properly; it was my responsibility to take the correction and grow instead of leave in offense. I submitted my heart and continued to grow. I've had many opportunities to be offended by my husband and other leaders who've corrected my actions. Discipline isn't pleasant in the moment, but it produces the peaceable fruit of righteousness. I have so much fruit in my life today because of pruning, correction, and my response to grow. There is no shortcut!

As leaders, Gary and I have also had to correct situations with others. Just as Paul experienced with Barnabas, it can be agonizing. You may not want to discipline your children, for example, but you also recognize that God has entrusted you with their lives. Every leader—from CEOs and pastors to parents—will give an account before the Lord Jesus for their leadership or lack thereof.

In the last days, people will not endure sound doctrine, but will listen to voices that tell them what they *want* to hear instead of what they *need* to hear. Leaders will give an account for their souls whether they spoke the truth or pandered to the culture. I'd rather offend with truth than coddle people with a lie and cause them to miss heaven or a reward for obedience to the Word of God.

YOUR WORDS REVEAL YOUR HEART, SHOWING WHAT YOUR ATTITUDE IS TOWARD THOSE WHOM GOD HAS PLACED IN YOUR LIFE AND OVER YOUR GROWTH.

What are you saying about your spouse, your pastor, your boss, or your coworkers? Your words reveal your heart, showing what your attitude is toward those whom God has placed in your life and over your growth. Words of hatred, animosity, or division grant authority to Satan to gain a place to enter into your relationships, health, and finances. *"By your words you will be justified, and by your words you will be condemned"* (Matthew 12:37 ESV).

Unless we repent, God has no power to overcome that which we say about our life. Watch your words, especially when you are frustrated, tired, and under pressure, when the enemy will try to make you take offense. Instead stay positive in your attitude about yourself and others by trusting God, even when things don't look good. A critical spirit can destroy relationships and your future. Instead of rehearsing a list of things going wrong for you, speak God's Word. Don't talk down your spouse, work, or the church. All of this is vanity! Scripture encourages us not to follow Hollywood, its stars, and other celebrities, but to shine like stars ourselves by watching our life and words.

> *Do everything without grumbling or arguing, so that you may become blameless and pure, "children of God without fault in a warped and crooked generation." Then you will shine among them like stars in the sky as you hold firmly to the word of life.* (Philippians 2:14–16)

> *He will make your righteous reward shine like the dawn, your vindication like the noonday sun.* (Psalm 37:6)

TRUST GOD TO DEAL WITH LEADERS

Our leaders are only human—they can make mistakes and have the wrong intentions or motives. So what do you do when mistreated or misunderstood? Lean on God to vindicate you! Trust God to reveal the truth to the leaders or authorities in your life, or give you wisdom on how to deal with a difficult person. You decide to do what is right in every situation. Give those in leadership over you the benefit of the doubt. There are often issues and pressures you do not see or understand.

I have found that after every pressure-filled test the enemy sends to derail, the Father rewards, comforts, and promotes us if we stay the course. God will even move in a fire or an earthquake to judge those who are unfairly treating His people. So don't grow weary in doing right, for in due season you will reap the harvest. Don't you dare quit! You are about to see His blessing in your life and relationships.

GIVE THOSE IN LEADERSHIP OVER YOU THE BENEFIT OF THE DOUBT. THERE ARE OFTEN ISSUES AND PRESSURES YOU DO NOT SEE OR UNDERSTAND.

Today maybe you are not right with God or the authority He has placed in your life. Maybe you are discouraged and feel like just giving up. God understands, but He's the answer, not the problem. He's not looking for perfection, but rather those who are humble enough to admit their need for Him, who will humbly follow Him. The cause of God will triumph through all the weaknesses and failures of His people. Our defeats are temporary and the celebration of our enemies is brief.

Forgetting what is behind and straining toward what is ahead, I press on toward the goal to win the prize for which God has called me heavenward in Christ Jesus. (Philippians 3:13–14)

Persevering in faith, not past faith, is the path to glory. Take up your cross, follow Jesus, and lean on Him.

From that deep intimacy with God will come great authority, resulting in supernatural exploits. God is moving in this hour of pressure. Let's keep our hearts steadfast and right, staying focused on Jesus, the King of Kings and Lord of Lords.

16

IT'S WORTH IT

In Florida during the 1920s and 1930s, Banyan trees were planted beside homes during the Spanish Mediterranean revival in architecture. These beautiful trees become massive and put out new shoots, forming new trunks. They create an amazing home to many birds and incredible shade and splendor for those lucky enough to have one.

I am an ocean girl and have always preferred being in the water to sunning on the shore. Years back, when the economy was down, I consistently poured through foreclosure and auction sites with a dream of one day owning a beach home. After a few years, thanks to a blessing from the Lord, we were able to purchase one of these Spanish revival homes featuring a fabulous Banyan tree more than seventy-five years old. Equal to the charm of the house is the big banyan tree, making a perfect jungle effect and barrier between us and a neighboring property.

We *ooohhhed* and *aaahhhed* over the tree, as did our family and friends. Eventually, we visited our beach home during the spring and discovered that our beautiful tree had made a huge mess on the patio and back courtyard. Leaves had fallen everywhere! And then berries began to drop—tens of thousands of them!

Our majestic shade tree had a downside. Part of the time, we adored it, yet the longer we owned the property, the more tempting it became to focus on the negative aspects of our tree. This gorgeous tree had not changed, but after closer inspection, its flaws became apparent and competed with its splendor.

Isn't that just like relationships? We admire the differences, the beauty of another person, and their individual personal traits that make them who they are. We are overtaken with the glory in them, the God-breathed creation, but the more we see them, the more we find fault. Their positive attributes haven't changed… but we have magnified the negative ones, failing to esteem all the attractive differences and qualities that we found charming and unforgettable.

IN LONG-TERM RELATIONSHIPS, SOME SEASONS CAN BE MESSY, BUT THE SPLENDOR IS WORTH IT.

In long-term relationships, some seasons can be messy—just like we realized with the banyan tree—but the splendor is worth it. I tried to picture our yard without the tree and honestly, it would be boring, just another lot in the neighborhood peering into a neighboring yard. The banyan sets our yard apart.

Why is it so hard to stay focused on the positive aspects of people once we discover what we consider to be their flaws?

For a relationship to withstand the pressures and messy aspect of life, there must be commitment, trust, and forgiveness. Commitment to an imperfect person—recognizing that we aren't perfect either—is key to becoming comfortable enough to be ourselves. It's a great comfort to know that although we are all flawed, someone is deeply committed to seeing the best in us. Love believes the best. (See 1 Corinthians 13:4–7.)

It's nice to know that even though we may be going through a tough season, there's someone who believes in us and is committed to see us through to the next season. They've seen us at our best and at our worst and they still choose to love us. That's the beauty of commitment in relationships. There's a beautiful shade and a quiet place of rest underneath its branches.

AMANDA'S STORY

Amanda Lenhart's story parallels mine in so many ways. Amanda grew up in a Christian home, where she witnessed the power of God, but after seeing her young cousin die and her brother develop a drug addiction, she decided that although she knew God was real, He wasn't good.

When entering her third year of law school, she was hired by a large, prestigious law firm after her bar exam. "One of the first pieces of advice I was given by a female partner was not to display pictures of my family in my office so that I would not be perceived as weak," she recalls.

Amanda worked as a successful trial attorney for more than fourteen years. "While I never openly criticized Christianity or God, no one would have ever expected that I had once known the Lord," she says. "I developed an abrasive, acerbic, sarcastic nature, and was quickly given the nickname 'Ice Queen.'"

AS A SUCCESSFUL TRIAL ATTORNEY, AMANDA CONSIDERED WOMEN "TO BE MOSTLY JEALOUS, BACKSTABBING GOSSIPS WHO WEREN'T REMOTELY FUNNY."

Although the firm was big, Amanda didn't have many friendships or working relationships with women. "On my very first day at work," she says, "I was told that I would be working in a group of all men. I jokingly responded, 'Good! I hate women and they hate me.' I did not work with women other than my secretary and I liked it that way. I considered women to be mostly jealous, backstabbing gossips who weren't remotely funny. Henceforth I became part of the boys' circle. Being isolated, I certainly did not have any Christian influence and I lost my heart for people, especially women."

Amanda wed years after starting her career and the marriage got off to a rocky start. She and her husband, Shawn, argued viciously and took their hurt out on each other. They wanted to have a baby, but with so much stress and strife in their relationship, they struggled to conceive. It finally happened and seven months into her pregnancy, Amanda was elected as a partner in her law firm—"the goal of every lawyer in private practice," she says. Amanda remembers:

> I loved being pregnant. And I loved every second of being with my newborn son, including staying up all night with him. I struggled with returning to work during the course of my maternity leave. By the end of it, I was truly in mourning. Everybody said, "You can't give up your partnership," "You must at least try it out," and "You will get used to leaving your kids at day care." But I never got used to it. I remembered my mom always being at home when we got off the bus, every day during the summer, taking me to dance class, making dinner. Mom stuff. That was the kind of mother I wanted to be. Then, six months later, the economy tanked, the banking industry was imploding, and financial institutions were begging for bailouts. My husband was a banker at that time, so I felt the pressure to continue earning for our family. At that time, we had a high mortgage, among other expenses, that kept me in bondage to my career. So I plugged away, operating out of straight-up fear.

After two miscarriages and more pain in their marriage, Amanda became pregnant with their second child—a true miracle since she was dangerously losing weight from disordered eating, too much exercise, and stress. After their second child was born, Amanda couldn't take the stress at her job anymore, so she quit. The family moved to Columbus, Ohio, where Shawn had been traveling a lot for work. Amanda stepped into a new role as the director of a large foundation, which allowed her to work from home and spend more time with her children. "Quitting the practice of law and staying home with my kids greatly softened me as a person and took the pressure off of me—huge factors in repairing our marriage," she says.

That was just the beginning of the changes in their life. The couple had an incredible encounter with God, and they began attending Faith Life Church every week. Shortly afterward, Amanda felt the call to be a stay-at-home mom and homeschool her children. It seemed like a crazy idea after coming from such a prestigious career, but Amanda and Shawn knew that God was calling them to do it.

"While it can be challenging, we have never been happier," Amanda says. "My relationships with my boys are strong, they are closely bonded, they are not subjected to false teachings and philosophies of teachers or peers, and they are taught in a loving environment by me. Above all, they are being taught that Jesus is Lord. They go directly to God with their prayers."

Amanda's life and heart completely changed. She traded the world's system of success for something so much better—God's system!

The thing that blows my mind is that God had His vision for my life all along even when my husband and I were in rebellion and living for ourselves. And what I had dreamt did not even touch the scale for what God had in store for us. He always had us in His hands; never were we left or forsaken. I've learned to be sensitive to the voice of God, pursue those dreams and visions that God has given me and have the courage to follow where He leads, even if it is in an area to which I am not accustomed or feel that I am not qualified. I have also learned not to be swayed by the world. If I had listened to what my colleagues and even friends were telling me, I would have stayed in my career. I had a person literally calculate how much money I've "missed out on" not working. If I had listened to the fear of relying on a single income or losing my independence, I would have been miserable and my children would have been raised by the world. All of the baggage that my husband and I brought into our marriage is gone. It has been replaced by His love. He is the center of our marriage and family. I now have a peaceful home with my husband, working together, with godly order, where my husband is the spiritual leader. I now trust that my husband is led by the Holy Spirit, has an abundance of wisdom, and will provide and protect our family. This has allowed me to trust in my husband as he trusts God. It has eliminated the need to control him or stir up strife to nurture the fear that tried to control me. The Bible instructs wives "to submit to their husbands as to the Lord as the husband is the head of the wife as Christ is the head of the church." I don't know whether this comes naturally to most women, but it didn't come naturally to me. Only God could have made this change in my heart! Now I feel like I am finally living my true and authentic identity. While an extreme departure from the message the enemy wants women to hear—take care of yourself, belittle men, control men—serving your husband is to be like Christ. The kingdom of God is diametric to the earth where the first become last, the wise foolish, and the poor inherit the earth. God is completing the work He began in me. I now know my God-given purpose is to make Jesus my everything, put Him first, be a godly wife to my husband, and a godly mother to my children. I am no longer called to forsake my family by pursuing selfish ambition. I am obeying the call that God put on my life as a child—to preach the gospel to all nations, make disciples of men and women, heal the sick, raise the dead, cast out demons, set the captives free, and destroy the works of the devil every day. I have claimed the spiritual blessing and inheritance my parents laid up for me in prayer and deed.

GOD HAS A PLAN FOR YOUR LIFE, AND IT IS SO MUCH BETTER THAN THE COUNTERFEIT PICTURE OF SUCCESS THE CULTURE IS TRYING TO SELL.

Amanda's message is one that Satan doesn't want women to hear. It's the message that set me free years ago, and I believe it has the power to set every woman free if she will listen. God has a plan for your life, and it is so much better than the counterfeit picture of success the culture is trying to sell. Nasty gets us nowhere! Women and men *can* succeed together. *And the journey is worth it.*

RELATIONSHIPS ARE MESSY

Gary and I have a two-seat bicycle that we love to ride on our quaint country roads. He gets his workout in and I get his undivided attention for half an hour while I talk and *kind* of work out in the back. Ha!

Gary has loved bicycling for years and he has always wanted to complete what's called a *century*, a hundred-mile bike ride. Despite not being in the best shape, we decided we were going to complete one on our tandem bike. We signed up for the hundred-mile bike ride around Lake Tahoe, California. We had never been to Lake Tahoe before, but it was advertised as "America's Most Beautiful Bike Ride," so I was all for it!

I pictured this really fun, daring, romantic day of adventure... but I couldn't have been more wrong. You see, when we signed up to bike around Lake Tahoe, we thought it was fairly flat terrain around a lake. I pictured this nice easy bike ride, maybe stopping for a few picnics along the way.

We didn't know Lake Tahoe is surrounded by *mountains*.

Isn't that just how it is in our relationships? You naively think you're going to have this perfect, easy life together. No disagreements. All good times. You don't think about what it's going to be like when you have to bike up a seven-mile stretch of mountain road hitched to this other person on your bike.

Relationships are messy.

Gary and I realized we were in trouble as we drove the steep mountains we would be biking the next day, but we were committed to finishing that century ride. We drove across the United States in an RV to make it happen. We just *had* to do it.

On the day before the bike ride, I was in line to register us and get our gear. The man standing in front of me turned around and asked the dreaded question. "So, how long have you been training?"

I forced a smile. "Well, we haven't really been training," I admitted. I could almost feel the judgment seeping from the people around me who had been training for months upon months, even up to a year. "We've done twenty miles on our tandem bicycle."

"You're doing this on a tandem bicycle?" he asked, appalled. "And you're going to go a hundred miles tomorrow?"

"Yeah, my husband and I are doing it together."

"You're crazy!" he exclaimed. "You might as well throw in the towel right here! There's no way you're doing a hundred miles. I've been training and getting in shape for this, and I can only do the seventy-two-mile route."

I had to stand in line by that man for thirty minutes and listen to him tell me how there was no way Gary and I could accomplish this bike ride. He was much younger and more athletic than us, so it was intimidating. But when someone tells me I can't do something, it only motivates me more. I committed to crossing that finish line, even if only to prove this man wrong.

WHEN SOMEONE TELLS ME I CAN'T DO SOMETHING, IT ONLY MOTIVATES ME MORE.

When I finally got up to the registration table, the lady asked, "Are you sure the hundred-mile route is what you want to do?"

"Yes," I said with as much confidence as I could muster. Which wasn't much.

The morning finally came, and we started the ride. As we got farther into it, we started hitting some steep hills. Watching the stretches of steep roads spreading far ahead of us, I realized how impossible coming back appeared to be. It was miles and miles of inclines. We were already tired, and we'd already gone much farther than we ever had before.

Now, up until this point, Gary had been doing the majority of the work. I was sitting on the back, videoing on my phone, and comfortably matching my feet to the rhythm he was setting. If you've ever ridden on a tandem bike before, you know how easy it is for the person in the back to look like they're pedaling hard… but they're not. Ha!

By the time we arrived at the lunch stop, Gary was pale and spent; he sat down and he didn't want to eat. I could tell that he was getting too tired to go on, and we still had miles of mountain road ahead of us. I went into my *prayer closet*, which happened to be the portable restroom there, and I began to pray out loud, forgetting that I wasn't in the privacy of my home. I usually pace when I pray intensely, but there was only room to sway back and forth as I pleaded, "God, please help us! Give us the grace to do this!"

When I marched out of there, the people around it stared at me. A man standing by said, "Are you all right?"

I guess I had been praying a little louder than I thought!

I returned to Gary, determined to get us back on the road and to the finish line. I felt God's grace on me.

"I don't know, Drenda…" he mumbled weakly.

"Don't say anything. We're going to be fine."

I got him to stand up, walk around, and then get back on the bike. Off we went again! This time, I pedaled harder. We finally hit eighty-three miles. The only problem was that the next eleven miles were straight up the worst climb of the entire bike ride. We were so close to one hundred miles, yet so far away. But how could we stop so close to our dream?

A MALE SPECTATOR INSULTED GARY BY SAYING, "SHE MUST BE THE ATHLETE IN THE FAMILY."

Both of us were exhausted, Gary was dehydrated, and we struggled mentally to go on. He stretched out on the side of the road, resting and rehydrating, as I walked in circles, keeping my legs moving and trying not to lose faith. Then a male spectator insulted Gary by saying, "She must be the athlete in the family." In that moment, I knew that although my man was down, he was definitely not out. It was my turn to help him finish his dream. So I did what we women know how to do best: I appealed to his manhood ever so gently, offering to push the bike up the hill and encouraging him to catch up with me when he was able. That got his attention!

Gary immediately stood and got back in the race. Riding again, I told Gary how awesome he is—which he is!—and cheered him on. We peddled as never before. I kept saying, "Once we get to the top of this hill, we will coast almost the entire way to the finish line." I prayed for wind, for anything to help us make those last miles.

When we reached the mountaintop, a surge of joy hit us both, and we flew down faster than I could imagine, going forty-five miles an hour on the steep, winding road. I closed my eyes, trusted my husband to steer, and prayed even harder, but I wasn't about to tell this man to slow down after what he had accomplished.

We finished that race. We passed many of the cyclists who had taunted us because we had more momentum going downhill with two on one bike. We crossed the finish line to cowbells, shouts, and our waiting family's cheers. That was a great moment for Gary and me. We got off that bike, hugged each other, and broke into tears. We praised one another. As we embraced, I could feel our hearts beating as one. We were so proud of each other. We'd worked as a team, completed something that at first seemed to be impossible, and finished ahead of many of the naysayers who had passed us as we struggled on mile eighty-three. *The race was worth it!*

It was much like the journey we have traveled together through life, starting out as a naive couple, raising children, going through dreams and disappointments, and growing love, encouragement, teamwork, and a deep respect and caring for each other because of the many miles traveled as one. Relationships are messy, but the journey is so worth it. Life is better when we succeed together!

RELATIONSHIPS ARE MESSY, BUT THE JOURNEY IS SO WORTH IT. LIFE IS BETTER WHEN WE SUCCEED TOGETHER!

HAILEY FRAZIER'S STORY

When I was a little girl, I put a cutout photo of a model under my pillow and would pray that God would make me beautiful so that I could be loved. Because of my abusive childhood and lack of identity, I would grow up to make poor decisions for my future. I was barely an adult when I married a man who challenged everything I knew about God. He led me to question God so much that I turned my back on Him. We had a son and before the baby was even one year old, our marriage was close to ending. After staring down the barrel of a gun held by my alcoholic, unfaithful spouse, I knew it was over. I went into my closet, fell on my knees, and told

God, "I am *not* a bad person. I try to do good and be good. But my life is empty, painful, and hopeless. God, *why* does my life look like this?" And as clear as anything, God told me, "Because you are choosing *this* life and *this* man, over the *life* and *man* that I have for you, I cannot bless you."

I took my baby and left with nothing but a car, a suitcase, and five dollars to my name. I spent my son's first Christmas and birthday in a women's safe house. I was convinced that no one could ever love a young, divorced, single mom. I felt so broken. All I wanted was to give my son a family and a good life.

I spent the next four years working on myself. During this time, my father and *bonus-mom* introduced me to the Keesees' teachings on how God's kingdom works. I watched their entire life changing dramatically—and I wanted mine to do the same. Every day, my father would encourage me by speaking guidance and God's word into my life; he also gave me lots of the Keesees' CDs. I began to fill my life with God's love and Word. Through this, He began to restore my broken relationship with my parents and my heart. I knew that because I believed in Christ, all of God's promises applied to me too. (See 1 Peter 2:9.) I realized I had to become the person God created me to be, in order to receive who He created for me. I started speaking over my life, and asked God to send the man that He had for me.

A friend named Timo reappeared in my life and showed significant interest in me, my heart, and life. He had since relocated to Europe as a photographer. Soon, we were talking every day. We talked for hours about our lives and God's Word. It wasn't long before I began to fall in love with this man. We hadn't even kissed or held hands!

Finally Timo decided to fly me to Europe so we could have a proper date and spend time together. By the end of that incredible trip to see Paris and the Swiss Alps, we both knew we *couldn't* do life without each other. He decided to fly back to Tennessee to meet my family and son. He was an instant fit and felt like the perfect puzzle piece in my life!

Soon, Timo brought me back to the countryside of France for a photo shoot. He had a gorgeous ball gown for me to wear and drove us to the most massive castle I have ever seen, Château De Chambord. After an hour of Timo taking photos, I turned around for another shot when he knelt on the ground and proposed to me, telling me I was everything he'd ever prayed for, that I made his life whole.

After a beautiful wedding in Nashville, we moved to Europe, where I studied fragrance and felt artistry. Now, a couple years later, happier than I've ever been, we have moved back to Tennessee and I have a successful clothing and fragrance brand based in Nashville and Paris, H. Lane Design.

My marriage to Timo works because he didn't put me on a pedestal like the world says he is supposed to; instead, he completed a missing part of me. Being in each other's lives made us the *best* version of ourselves. Neither of us is greater; we're a team! Every single day, I wake up and look at this incredible life we are building and I know it would not be possible without God. I could never deny that!

TREACHEROUS TIMES

We are living in treacherous times and the days are evil. Schism and division keep us from the glory of God filling our churches and overflowing into the world. Yet these are the days that God's Word says the glory of the Lord will cover all. For us to see the glorious church, we must heal our fractures and unite, women and men succeeding together for the kingdom of God.

WE MUST HEAL OUR FRACTURES AND UNITE, WOMEN AND MEN SUCCEEDING TOGETHER FOR THE KINGDOM OF GOD.

We are living in the hour in which God desires to pour out His Spirit on all the earth, through His sons and daughters, but it will not happen unless women and men under His voice are unified for one purpose. We cannot fulfill our God-ordained destiny without both working together as it was in God's original plan before the fall. God began with a family, *male and female He made them.* He told them to be fruitful, multiply, and replenish the earth. This is spiritual as well as natural. In this hour, we are to multiply His kingdom with signs and wonders and reveal God to the world.

> *There is neither Jew nor Gentile, neither slave nor free, nor is there male and female, for you are all one in Christ Jesus.* (Galatians 3:28)

People are flawed and imperfect, but treating each other with nastiness is never the answer. It seems that in the last decade, women and men have especially learned to treat each other with contempt. I must say that we females have learned to fight dirty. Call it retribution if you will… but does that make it excusable? There are *good* men out there and the flawed ones do not negate God's plan for us to get along. We were created with equality but very different. That's a good thing! We both bring something beautiful and clever to the table when we work together.

Nasty has gotten us nowhere. It's only resulted in confusion and brokenness for both of us. Alcoholism is soaring among women and statistically they're less happy than ever. Men are perceiving women as untrustworthy and are no longer choosing marriage or long-term commitments. Children are committing suicide at a greater rate than at any time in history. We have to stop being nasty before we destroy everything, including each other and civilization. We *can* succeed together… and much of our happiness depends on it. Working together won't always be easy, but I believe with the grace of God backing you, it *is* possible.

OUR CANA WEDDING

Leaving Jerusalem and traveling the bumpy road to Cana by bus, I was fighting disappointment. Before we left, I had asked Gary about the day's travel schedule just as he was heading down to breakfast and I was stepping out of the shower in our small hotel room. We had worked nonstop for months and had met up in New Jersey, coming from two different cities, to head to Israel for eight days.

The tour began after an overnight flight. It was our third morning, but we were still feeling jet lag from the six-hour time difference. I never got an answer about the schedule, so I threw on a tracksuit and decided to forgo doing much to my hair or makeup. I joined Gary downstairs for a Middle Eastern breakfast of hummus, cucumber salad, and bread before loading up on the bus.

On the ride, our guide began to share the day's plans. "We are headed to Cana and for those of you who wish, we have a ceremony planned where you may renew your wedding vows."

"Oh, no!" I said aloud. This was the only event I had really planned an outfit for and I was wearing a blue tracksuit! I glanced around the bus; every other woman looked more dressed up than me. I had made an effort to dress nicely the two previous days and now we were headed to Cana! I didn't want to renew my vows in *this*!

I was aggravated for a moment that Gary hadn't checked the schedule. I told him I had a special blouse I had planned to wear to renew our vows and I was disappointed.

"You can just wear it to supper later," he reasoned.

Then I thought, *How silly of me to be bothered about such a small matter.* Gary didn't care, why should I? I had seen couples disagree about minor issues at our marriage conferences and I knew this qualified as one.

It's just a tour bus not our wedding day, I thought. *After thirty-eight years, this is what you get!* We were tired, but still happily married. I was not going to let my outfit bother me. Beautiful weather with sunny skies and a slight breeze made me think, *I could be home in the snow, working, but I'm in the Holy land with my husband… but I packed that blouse thinking how romantic it would be to renew our vows… No!* I snapped out of it and decided to forget about the pretty cream lace top with belled sleeves. The blue tracksuit would work just fine!

We walked the courtyards to the Church at Cana and I saw everything from full-length wedding gowns and bridal parties to shorts and T-shirts. As we entered the modest room adjoining the wedding church and settled in, the man next to me pointed out that the cloth-covered table in the center was actually a pool table, for one of the pool pockets was showing. I started to laugh. I could picture the Franciscan sisters or monks playing pool and quickly throwing a tablecloth back on before anyone arrived. I kept laughing as I pointed it out to Gary. My tracksuit and tennis shoes weren't so bad after all.

AS WE RENEWED OUR VOWS, WE BOTH REALIZED THAT TENDERNESS TOWARD EACH OTHER WAS EXACTLY THE BALM OUR HEARTS NEEDED.

The pastor instructed couples to stand and face each other. "Husbands repeat after me…" Looking into my eyes, Gary began to repeat his vows, "I promise to always be tender-hearted toward you…" He slowed and his eyes watered as did mine. We both were weary from dealing with problems, people, and outside pressures. At the same time, we both realized that tenderness toward each other was exactly the balm our hearts needed. The look in his eyes reminded me of our actual wedding day when he stopped during our vows, tearfully pausing a moment to complete them. Later, his cousin would make fun of him, but I knew how seriously he valued our day and how long he had trusted God for his wife. Remembering, I was touched deeply in my heart and forgot the tracksuit. All I saw was Gary, God's faithfulness, and the life we built together—*our* life and our family.

Afterward, Gary hurried to purchase the memorial wedding certificate, and as we signed it together, he told me how special this day was to him. Jesus turned a rough ride in a tracksuit into a tender marriage moment we both needed.

At times, I still find myself thinking back to when I was that seventeen-year-old girl lying on her bed after an abortion, broken and tempted to take her own life. She was so ashamed. So scared. So lost.

To be honest, she didn't deserve anything. She had made too many mistakes and taken too many wrong turns. If anyone deserved a healthy relationship, or a beautiful family, surely it wasn't that girl who encouraged her friends to get abortions and hated men. Anyone but her.

Put your hope in the LORD, for with the LORD is unfailing love and with him is full redemption. (Psalm 130:7)

But God… God had a better plan for my life—not one I deserved, but one that He bought for me with His very life. He took my sin, my shame, my hurt, and my bitterness, and He turned my life into something beautiful.

And He'll do the same for you.

Today, I marvel at how God has brought my life full circle. I have attended over seventy births, cheering on women as they take on the great call to be a mother. I have been an advocate for marriage and family all over the world for over two decades, writing books, speaking at events, and ministering on television. I have shown young girls that there's a path besides abortion, and have helped young mothers educate their children at home.

Luke 1:45 says, *"Blessed is she who has believed that the Lord would fulfill his promises to her!"* And so I have been!

Please know my heart. I'm not saying any of this to brag about myself. God took the area where I had the most shame, where I made the most mistakes, and He used me for His good. I want you to understand today that no matter how many mistakes you've made, no matter what attacks the enemy has brought against you, no matter what lies you've believed, *God restores!*

Today, I look back on my life, and I am in awe of the work God has done in both of us. I thought I knew what happiness was as a young girl—I thought if I hardened myself to people, I would never be hurt and I could be an independent woman. God knew what I wanted wasn't what I *needed.* What I have discovered through the years is that happiness only comes when we are vulnerable and open to others, and we all come together as a team.

> There is no such thing as a self-made man. You will reach your goals only with the help of others.
> —George Shinn

Gary and I have had our ups and downs, adventures, and surprises along the way, but I am so happy we made the decision to do it together. We truly are stronger and better working as a team. As a young girl, I set out to discover the truth—and I know I've found it. God's system for women and men succeeding together is so much better than the world's system of rebellion and blame.

Working together isn't always easy, but *it's worth it.* The journey together is more beautiful than words can describe.

ABOUT THE AUTHOR

Drenda Keesee is passionate about bringing people into spiritual, emotional, and relational wholeness. She is an internationally sought-after speaker and is known for her high-energy, tell-it-like-it-is approach to life's problems.

When life doesn't go as planned, most people sacrifice happiness for survival. Drenda lived that way for nine painful years, struggling to navigate marriage and parenting as she and her husband, Gary, fell into deep financial distress. They cried out to God, and what He showed them radically changed their lives forever. Now Drenda is on a mission to help people find happiness and unlock the secrets to God's kingdom that turned their dreams into their reality.

Drenda is the television host of the *Drenda* show, an international daily broadcast, and co-host of *Fixing the Money Thing*.

As the creators of several successful businesses and the founders of Faith Life Now, Drenda and Gary produce worldwide conferences, media, and practical resources to equip people for success in their faith, family, and finances. They also pastor Faith Life Church in New Albany, Ohio.

Drenda has been sharing spiritual and practical principles for success and happiness for over twenty-five years. She holds a master's degree in Christian Counseling from Logos University and an honorary Doctorate of Divinity from CICA International University and Seminary. She is the author of thirteen books, including *The New Vintage Family, Better Than You Think,* and *She Gets It!*

Recognized as one of Ohio's Top 20 Women You Should Know by Columbus Radio Group, Drenda has appeared as a special guest on numerous shows, including *Enjoying Everyday Life* with Joyce Meyer, *Joni Table Talk, Marcus and Joni, America Stands, Victorython Programmers' Event,* and more. She has been a featured speaker at various nationwide events and has ministered throughout the world.

Drenda's personal stories of struggle and overcoming resonate with people, and she is known for her ability to inspire, empower, and encourage others to embrace God's best for their lives.

Drenda and Gary have five children—Amy, Timothy, Tom, Polly, and Kirsten—all of whom serve alongside them in business and ministry.